Related Events to the Second Coming of the Christ

THE
NEW WORLD
ORDER

Volume 10

MICHAEL W. DEWAR

Copyright © 2023 by Michael W. Dewar
THE NEW WORLD ORDER

eBook ISBN:979-8-9883484-7-4
Paperback ISBN: 979-8-9883484-6-7

Published by Dwelling Place Publishers
Brooklyn, New York 11236
United States of America

DPSCleansing.com

All rights reserved solely by the author. The author guarantees all contents are original and do not infringe upon the legal rights of any other person or work. No part of this book may be reproduced in any form without the permission of the author.

Unless otherwise indicated, Bible quotations are taken from The Holy Bible, New International Version(NIV). Copyright © 1973, 1978, 1984 by International Bible Society; The New King James Version (NKJV); The Holy Bible, King James Version(KJV); and The Holy Bible, New Living Translation(NLT). Copyright © 1996 by Tyndale House Publishers, Inc.

Dedication

To my beloved sister and brother Joyce and Gilbert, may your life continue to be healthy, blessed, and flourishing. And may you be residents in the eternal city of our Lord Jesus Christ.

"By establishing a relationship with Jesus Christ now, we secure our own dwelling place in new world to come and in its capital city, the New Jerusalem." Michael W. Dewar, author

CONTENTS

PREFACE vii

INTRODUCTION 9

CHAPTER 1 13
THE RATIONALE FOR A NEW WORLD ORDER 13

CHAPTER 2 25
THE NATURE OF THE COMING NEW CREATION 25

CHAPTER 3 39
THE PEOPLE OF THE NEW CREATION 39

CHAPTER 4 53
ANGELS AND THE NEW WORLD ORDER 53

CHAPTER 5 61
THE GOVERNMENT OF THE NEW WORLD ORDER 61

CHAPTER 6 75

THE OUTSIDERS	75
CHAPTER 7	89
SECURING YOUR NEW JERUSALEM DWELLING NOW	89
REFERENCES	101
OTHER BOOKS BY THIS AUTHOR	103
ABOUT THE AUTHOR	107
CONTACT AND REVIEW	109

PREFACE

Welcome to the final volume in this series of ten. Let me hope you are seizing the opportunity to read all ten books in the series, even conduct Bible study groups in your home, at the office, or at church. Sharing these small volumes with relatives and friends can be a fruitful ministry, indeed. They can certainly enrich and inform your spiritual life. Some have bought all ten paperbacks at once; I will share a link at the end where you can do that.

Let me take this opportunity to thank all of you who will or have already purchased the series in part or in whole; you are my partners in ministry getting this information out to the body of Christ, and perhaps to those who have not yet had a salvation experience with Jesus Christ.

Think of walking down main street in the New Jerusalem and run into a few people that you have known; they are there all because one day you handed them a book that led them to Jesus

Christ. You did a kind act, you sowed a seed in their lives, and that made all the difference in their eternal destiny.

Love, kindness, compassion, forgiveness are seeds with tremendous power to change lives. These seeds of the word and from the word of God should not be underestimated, especially when intentionally sown in the lives of others. Paul the apostle said, I plant and Apollos water, but God gives the increase (1Cor.3:6-9). Jesus invites all of us to be sowers of good seeds (Matt.13:18-21).

Let me also thank those of you that have written reviews on each book, frankly I quietly wish everyone of you would write an honest review of each book in the series on Amazon or wherever you bought your copy or copies. I will leave a link at the end of the book that will take you to Amazon's review page or you can copy and paste it.

Finally, let me thank all of you who took the time to submit feedback to improve these volumes; I really welcome those as well. You can email your feedback to me at cs@dpscleansing.com or from my website at :dpscleansing.com.

INTRODUCTION

This is the final volume in a series of ten. Perhaps, you are starting with this volume, so let me use the first part of this introduction to bring you up to speed. If you have already read the previous volumes in the series, you may want to refresh your memory or skip a couple pages ahead, that's okay; either way you are ahead of the game. The next half a dozen paragraphs are a kind of brief review to help the new readers who are starting here.

According to the author's understanding of the Word of God, the "New World Order" is at least a thousand years in the future. But don't be fooled thinking you have time, the countdown to world tomorrow has already begun. And it can accelerate in the blink of an eye with that event Bible scholars refer to as "The Rapture" (see Volume 1).

In other words, before you know what hit you, you could be standing before the judgment seat of Christ in heaven (see Vol.2). But relax, you have the better of the deal, you are in heaven; no matter what happen from here you will not get thrown out of heaven by the Judge or anyone else.

But it is not going to be that good for some of your friends and acquaintances who did not make the trip to heaven with you; they are left behind on earth, and all hell will be breaking loose for the next seven years on earth. This time is called *The Great Tribulation* (see Volume 3).

As you count down to the near end of the Great Tribulation, you and millions of others will return to earth with Jesus; this is called, "The Second Coming of the Christ" (see Volume 5). Jesus is back on earth, and He has the ultimate war to fight against evil; it is called, Armageddon. It is the wicked nations against Christ (see Volume 6).

Christ is victorious, and with that victory He marches into Jerusalem, sits on the reestablished throne of King David, and rules over the earth in righteousness and justice. It will be a time of unprecedented peace and prosperity.

This thousand-year reign of Christ on earth and over the earth is called, The Millennium (see Volume 7). At the end of the Millennium will be "The Final Judgment." The wicked dead are resurrected and judged and disposed with Satan and his angels. Evil is wiped clean from God's creation (see Volume 9).

With evil vanquished from the creation, the Son hands off authority to the Father, the old world is destroyed, and "The New World Order" is established. We now invite you to come along as we explore this new world in this final volume.

The New World Order
This tenth and last volume in the series carries you through the closing chapters of the Bible. It is a weird feeling, not only to reach

INTRODUCTION

the end of the Bible, but the end of all things. The old order has ended! Everything you have grown to love, or hate has come to its end. We got rid of the Antichrist, the False prophet, all wicked people, demons, fallen angels, Satan, sickness, disease, and death.

It is weird to find yourself shouting good reddens when you see one angel arresting bad boy Satan, and later throwing him into the Lake of fire. Then in reflection hearing yourself saying, but that's the only devil we have; we don't know the one we are going to get. Shaking yourself back to reality, it dawn on you that is it, we are not going to get another devil. We don't need another one!

Then you turn around to see God getting rid of this old earth, and the old heaven too; everything is going up in flames. He creates a new heaven, a new earth, and a new capital city called, the New Jerusalem, and relocates His new home closer to earth to dwell with us humans (Rev.21:1-4). We are His family, and He has always wanted to dwell among us and that has now become a reality.

Emotionally and psychologically, the authorship of this final volume has moved me in a good way but beyond words to express. It generated mixed feelings of weirdness and excitement, frightful, yet joyful and wonderful and so intense, the physical body could hardly contain itself. It clarifies for me the verse that says flesh and blood cannot inherit the kingdom of God. It is intense!

Have you ever been transported into a movie you were watching, absorbed to the point of forgetting your physical surroundings? Well, those are the emotions felt writing about the end of all things old, and the beginning of all things new. I heard God said, "Behold, I am making all things new (Rev.21:5). He means, all things, a complete do over!

If you have never envisioned how God feels about us, and what He has in store for us, the closing four chapters of Revelation (19-22) with this final volume will give you a brief heart-pulsating preview. It is brief because most of the details are still classified. But there is enough here to get you excited beyond measure.

In Elisa E. Hewitt's classical hymn, "when we all get to Heaven, what a a day of rejoicing that will be!" there is a line that says, "Just one glimpse of Him in glory, will the toils of life repay." In other words, just to get one short look of Jesus will worth all you have suffered in this life. We will be getting more than a glimpse; we will be dwelling with Him in New Jerusalem and the new earth.

This volume on *The New World Order* discussed the themes raised in this introduction and more. May the reading of it edify, excite, and bless you as the writing of it did for the author.

CHAPTER 1

THE RATIONALE FOR A NEW WORLD ORDER

Some people will ask, why is a *New World Order* necessary? The old world seems just fine! Look at the majesty of Mount Everest, the grandeur of the Grand Canyon, the wonder of the mighty Pacific, the awe-inspiring Amazon River, the thundering Victoria's and Niagara Falls, there is no need to change all that, says the critic. Consider the serene, picturesque beauty of the Poconos Fall foliage, the variety of human cultures around the world, the exotic foods, and culinary delights we enjoy, why throw away all that for something new that we have not even tested, they protested.

It is true, most of us have not gotten around to explore and enjoy the old world yet; we have been too busy working and raising a family. We have four wonderful seasons, including seedtime and harvest time. These seasons are working fine; it would be a downright, crying shame to trade them in now for something new and unfamiliar. If you ask me, I say we keep the world we know, asserts one preacher; he was quoting another critic of the faith.

Others are saying, look at what we humans have done to the earth, we are the problem! The earth is soaked with the blood of our brothers and sisters through war and violence, holocaust, massacres, ethnic cleansing, slavery, disease, pollution, injustice, and greed. Give us a new world, and we will just make another ghetto out of it. We must learn to clean up this old world first! Yes, we should give it a thorough cleanup job, make it look like new. The problem is—they want to bring that about by human efforts alone.

But the decision to create a new world is not for the sons of Adam and daughters of Eve to make; they are tenants not owners. The Creator is the true landlord and owner. He did not consult angels of any rank when He created this old world, and I do not think He needs advice this time around.

Despite it is God's prerogative alone, He has given us His perspective or rationale as to why He is creating all things new. The details are classified, but the big picture He has revealed. This chapter explores the revelation of His rationale for creating not only "a new heaven and a new earth," but for making "all things new" (Rev.21:1-5). Why?

The answer rests in two fundamental reasons. First, though not out of God's control or took Him by surprise, *the first creation went contrary to God's perfect will.* You don't have to be a genius to see that. It a good thing He had a backup plan in place from the beginning; it is called, redemption. We are told that Jesus is the Lamb slain before the foundation of the word, but to humans, it happened in the fullness of time on a hill called, Calvary, outside Jerusalem (1Pet.1:18-20; Gal.4:4-5).

Second, the first creation has fallen and become desecrated. For these reasons, God has decided, not to just spruce up the old creation, but create a completely new world: new heaven, new earth, new capital city, all things new! We are exploring this rationale in this chapter to provide a clearer understanding of God's perspective as revealed in Scripture. The more we know God, the better able we are to give Him the honor, praise, and glory due to Him. We begin the discussion by trying to understand the nature and purpose of God in creation.

God Is Relational and Filial

In essence God is relational and filial in His Being. His purpose for creating humans is anchored in this relational and filial essence which provides us insight into His rationale for a new world order. In other words, the new world is the perfect home for His new and perfect family. If you still didn't get it, let's unpack this a little more.

God is relational within Himself; this is possible because of the triunity of God as Father, Son, and Holy Spirit (Matt.28:19-20). God is a family; a family has love relationship within itself. That unit needs nothing outside of itself to be fulfilled and satisfied. It is that pleasure within the unit that moves it to expand.

For example, to add children. A selfish, miserable person or couple rarely expand beyond themselves, and if they do, they rarely if ever build a happy family. It is a proven fact that twisted, dysfunctional individuals build twisted, unhappy, and dysfunctional families. From eternity, before there was a creation, God exists in perfect love relationship as a family.

Let's look at the triunity of God for a moment. But a word of caution first. We as finite mortals cannot fully comprehend God who is infinite; "God is incomprehensible but knowable."[1] What we know of God is what He chose to reveal to us about Himself. God reveals Himself in general in creation (Ps.19:1-6;Rom.1 18-20). He reveals Himself in uniquely making humans His image bearer; ultimately, He reveals Himself in the Lord Jesus Christ (Gen.1:26-28; Heb.1:1-4).

Furthermore, the revealed knowledge of God is progressive. Progressive, in the sense that God never reveals all He wants us to know about Him at once. Our little brains would explode into a million bits. So, we must assume an attitude of humility when we set out to talk about God. He is always in control, not us.

Back to the triunity of God (three in one). God presents Himself as One. "Hear, O Israel: The LORD our God, the Lord is one" (Deut.6: 4). But in this oneness, there is the Triune-Being who said, "Come let us make mankind, in our image, in our likeness..." (Gen.1:26).

Here we see the One speaking in a plural form. Yet, it is idolatrous, heretical, and blasphemous to say there are three Gods (Ex.20:1-6). Christianity firmly embrace One God, the triune God. You can spend three lifetimes trying to wrap your brain around this one and you will end up exactly where you started. So, let's accept the infinitude of God and move on.

The Godhead is the perfect family in perfect love relationship. Jesus said, "I am in the Father, and the Father is in me..." (John 14:10-11). In His high priestly prayer (John 17) Jesus not only speaks of the triunity of God, but He also speaks of becoming one with His people (vv.20-21). The Bible presents God to us as a love family (John 3:16; 1John 4:8). The material world, the creation, is God's way of extending His love family in a perfect environment where He Himself would dwell with them in perfect harmony. It's like a man acquiring a nice, safe place, builds a house, then moves his family in. Eden is about God creating a home and family in love as an extension of His family. But something went terribly wrong.

But first note that humans were created last, on the sixth day of creation (Gen.1:26-31). God creating a place for His family. The creation of Humans, therefore, was the crowning work of God's creation, according to the Psalmist (Ps.8: 4-9). Humans are the grand finale of God's creation work. The angelic population erupted with jubilant and applauding ovation to the Creator upon the completion of the creation. God speaks of it as the morning stars singing together, and the sons God shouting for joy (Job 38:4-7). In a similar way an angelic choir erupted in praise to God at the birth of our Lord Jesus (Luke 2:8-13).

Creation has only one group that holds a grudge against humans, and it is that Luciferian rebel group that lost their place in heaven and got thrown out (Isa.14:12-15; Ezek.28:13-15; Rev.12:1-9). Lucifer and his cohorts would make trouble for the family of God whom God gave governance or rulership over the earth.

The universe was created with earth in mind; the heavenly bodies make it possible to sustain life on earth. Earth was created with the expansion of God's love family in mind. It was created to accommodate humans as part of God's family, and as a place for God to grow His family and dwell among them. God dwelling in the

Paradise Garden with Adam and Eve was the beginning of a family that would fill the earth with its kind (Gen.1:26-28).

The very fact that the man and the woman were the image and likeness bearers of the Creator speaks to the fact that they were His offspring. It is natural that they would look to God as their parents. And I say, parents, because God speaks of Himself in the plural form. "Come let us make man in our image and likeness" (Gen.1:26). As we mortals are the image and likeness bearers of our parents who give us life; so, Adam and Eve bore the image and likeness of God in some unique way, despite God being incorporeal.

Furthermore, since all of us humans are the offspring of Adam and Eve, the God image and likeness is also transferred to us as well.

The Fall of man, therefore, was a family tragedy; God loss His family to an enemy, an intruder to the garden home of His children. The intruder pretended to be a harmless friend offering a different perspective to the parental directive God gave His children.

They were deceived. They ingested the forbidden fruit, thus poisoning themselves and resetting the genetic code of the race inside of them. The Luciferian virus infected them; they were taken captive. With eyes wide open, Adam and his lovely wife went straight off the cliff with the same rebel that started the rebellion in heaven. You may call this Lucifer's displaced aggression; he could not conquer the stronger, so he went for the weaker.

The parental family bond of fellowship with God was not just slightly fractured, it was broken. All humanity went off the rails with Adam and Eve for the race was in them. The prophet Isaiah says it right, "All we like sheep have gone astray, we have turned everyone to his own way" (Isa.53:6 KJV). Humankind became totally lost.

Redemption is God's pursuit to bring His family back to Himself. Jesus said, "The Son of Man came to seek and to save that which was lost" (Matt.18:11 KJV). The Bible is the unfolding of this love story of the Father's pursuit of His lost family. Humans were created in love and God set out to redeem them in love (John 3:16).

So, what we have seen with the fall of the man and his wife is the desecration of a family, the desecration of a race, and the desecration of creation. Sin is a contagious spiritual virus of death, carried on through biology of blood from generation to generation. In Adam all humans die, all have sinned and come short of the glory of God. The virus destroys love relationship between God and humans, and love relationship between humans and humans, as happened in the case of Adam and Eve with their God and Cain and Able as brothers (Gen.3-4). It is death: spiritual, relational, physical.

Here is the sum for the first point in God's rationale for wanting a new heaven and earth—the first creation went contrary to God's will in the sense that God loss His family to a rebel named Satan. We will look at the second rationale in the next section.

The Whole Creation Fell

First, the fall of humans was not an isolated event, quarantined to a local garden for a short time with no further effects. The tragedy of Eden was much more than the fall of two people from their loft position of privilege and grace. Just as the fall of Lucifer had consequences for the entire created order, the fall of humans had a similar impact upon the creation.

Second, the rebellion of Lucifer infected at least a third of the angelic population in heaven (Rev.12:3-4). His rebellion precipitated war in heaven which resulted in the expulsion of Lucifer and his cohorts. In contrast, the fall of Adam and Eve resulted in death, the corruption of the entire human race, and their expulsion from Paradise (Gen.3:22-24; Rom.5:12).

Third, just as Lucifer's sin desecrated things in heaven that the blood of animals could not sanctify, so the sin of Adam desecrated the human family, and the blood of animals could not remove it. Both things in heaven and earth had to be sanctified by the efficacy of Christ's blood of atonement. Jesus entered heaven, the true Holy of Holies, as the High Priest with His own blood (Heb.9:23-28).

Fourth, the Luciferian virus was contained in heaven but not contained to heaven. In other words, the virus did not spread to other angels; the expulsion of Lucifer and his cohorts took care of that. But the virus spread to earth, because that's where Lucifer ended up with his spiritual Ebola problem. Heaven knew the danger that this rebel would pose to the inhabitants of earth, for a verbal bulletin was issued warning earth of the dangers coming down to them. It says, "Woe to the inhabitance of the earth for Lucifer is gone down with great wrath" (Rev.12:12 KJV).

Lucifer came down angry and out for revenge. At the opportune time he took out his anger upon God's family in the Paradise Garden. He deviously coned Adam and his wife out of what would have been their inheritance and had them expelled from Paradise as he was expelled from heaven. He took over the rulership of earth from them, and setup himself as god over it (2 Cor.4:4).

Satan now have humans working for him, managing earth for the new owner. Yes, Satan is behaving as the owner; he is roaring and strutting around claiming to be the god of this world. He is owner without title deed; the Creator holds the title deed (Ps.24:1).

Satan at some point showed up at a conference where other angels were reporting to God—God asked him where he was coming from, he said from going to and from, up and down on the earth (Job 1:6-7). In other words, I am serving my real estate property your son Adam gave to me.

Satan deceived Adam and Eve out of what would have been their inheritance, and it appears he got it legally. Satan is now the chief leader of this world's system. Even Jesus calls him "the prince of this world" (John 12:31,14:30,16:11). Satan offered the kingdom of this world in all its glory as a bribe for Jesus to worship him, but Jesus refused his offer and run him off (Matt.4:8-11). The Bible tells us the whole world is under the control of Satan, the wicked one (1John 5:19). The apostle Paul refers to Satan as the prince who rules the atmospheric heaven and unbelievers are subjected to him; they are the children of disobedience (Eph.2:2).

But don't be fooled, Satan cannot bring rain or produce crops, give the lilies their beautiful coat or the rainbow its colors; he cannot provide the seasons for seedtime and harvest to feed humans, beast, birds, and other animals. All that is under God's control (Gen.8:22; Matt.6:28-34; 1Cor.3:6-9). Satan is a usurper, a killer, murderer, and destroyer, not an original thinker and creator. Jesus is the giver of "abundant life" (John 10:10b KJV).

Understand this—God did not give ownership of the earth to humans; He gave humans management rights and tenancy rights for a time (Gen.1:28-30, 2:15). That period of human management and tenancy ends with the Second Advent of Jesus Christ. If Adam had not fallen, perhaps, tenancy would have long ended. Satan knows his time is short, that he can only have control until then. Jesus has the title deed of the earth, the earth is the Lord's (Ps.24:1,

95:1-7). Jesus is given all authority in heaven and on earth (Matt.28:18; Rev.1:18). Satan will be arrested and disposed of (Rev.20:1-3,7-10).

Fifth, the fall of man in the Paradise Garden did not just corrupt Adam and his wife and the race of humans inside of them; the Fall corrupted the entire creation. The apostle Paul gives us the following insight into the far-reaching consequences of the Fall:

> For the creation was subjected to frustration, not by its own choice, but by the will of the one who subjected it in hope, that the creation itself will be liberated from its bondage to decay and be brought into the freedom and glory of the children of God. (Rom.8:20-21).

At the time of the Fall, Adam and his wife experienced the following: 1) the glory of God that covered them departed. 2) Their fellowship with the Creator was broken. 3)They became susceptible to sin, death, shame, and hiding. 4) The woman was punished with painful child-bearing, and 5) the man was sentenced to scratch out a living from a cursed earth until he dies and returns to it. 6) The man and his wife were finally expelled from their garden home (Gen.3:1-24). The Fall of man affects the entire created order.

The Fall brings the whole creation under a cause (Gen.3:17-19). The apostle Paul reminds us that "the whole creation travails in pain until now." The creation is subjected to bondage of corruption, decay, and death (Rom.8:18-29). The Fall kind of incapacitate our ability to be responsible "stewards of Eden," the earth.[2]

When God gets back His family fully through the process of redemption, the curse upon creation will be lifted (Rom.8:18-25).

But instead of just lifting the curse and renovating the old creation, which is used and desecrated with Lucifers fingerprints all over it, God has chosen to create a new heaven, a new earth, a new capital called, the New Jerusalem, the place of His dwelling. He has decided to relocate His new dwelling closer to earth to be with His new family (Rev.21-22). That is God's rationale for a new created order. It is His gift to human family and to Himself.

Summary

The fall of humankind in the Paradise Garden was not just a local event confined to one man and his wife in one place; it was a cosmic event involving the entire human race that was in Adam and his wife. It includes the desecration of the whole created order. It was also profoundly connected to the fall and expulsion of Lucifer from heaven to earth. The two events are by no means isolated.

When Lucifer got thrown out of heaven his rebellion was over in that location; there was no mechanism for the virus to spread further. If other angels were sympathetic to Lucifer, they did not join him; there was no further defection and expulsion.

But the rebellion for Lucifer was not over; it continues to this day. He carried the virus to earth and infected God's family in the *Paradise Garden*. Satan lied on God to the woman; she acting on that lie was the cause of her downfall and expulsion from Paradise.

Satan is not a straight shooter. He is an expert liar; lying is his native tongue (John 8:44). He lied to Eve about God, and he slandered Job to God, charging that Job was just serving God because God showered him with good things, that Job would curse

God to His face if the good things he enjoyed were taken away (Job 1:9-11). In colloquial language, God was just a sugar daddy to Job.

Lucifer's lie and fraud against God was not fully exposed to the principalities and the entire angelic population until Calvary. Satan had an innocent man framed and crucified. The Seed of the Woman, the Son of Man, the Son of God on the cross full exposed Satan's treachery to the understanding of the entire created order. The lifting up of Christ was the casting down of Satan.

The new world order will be pristine, holy, holy, holy; it will have nothing in it that Satan has touched. God will first get rid of Satan and all evils, then He will create all things new. Sin, suffering, death, hate, violence, war and all such former things will be gone forever from His creation.

The new world order will be a truly perfect environment for God people to enjoy for all eternity in their glorified state. "I am making everything new," says the Lord (Rev.21:5).

CHAPTER 2

THE NATURE OF THE COMING NEW CREATION

What is the new creation going to be like? What will be its true nature and its contents? This chapter seeks to answer these two broad questions. But again, the text of Scripture gives us a broad overview, but the details of this coming new world order no human eyes have ever seen, except what was conveyed to the apostle John in his apocalyptic vision (Rev.1:1-3).

But as a general matter, the Word of God states, "What no eye has seen, what no ear has heard, and what no human mind has conceived—the things God has prepared for those who love him—these are the things God has revealed to us by his Spirit" (1Cor.2:9-10). In other words, physical eyes have not seen the world to come, but by faith the people of God can see it clearly afar.

Visions of A Celestial City

The people of God under the Old Covenant, by faith speak of a new world order in in differing terms. It is said that Abraham made his home in the promised land like a stranger in a foreign country; he lived in tents, as did Isaac and Jacob, who were heirs with him of the same promise. "For he was looking forward to the city with foundations, whose architect and builder is God" (Heb.11:9-10).

This man of faith was anticipating much more than a man-made city with limited lifespan, but one that is eternal. Only the new world order will have such a city with eternal durability and majesty, a city build by God with many foundations (Rev.21:14).

Abraham, Isaac, Jacob, Moses, and people of like faith were seeking not just an earthly dwelling, but a heavenly country, a place better than the one they had left (Heb.11:15-16). It was promised to them, and by faith they could see it afar off. But they did not and will not inherit or occupy that heavenly city and country before their brothers and sisters of the New Covenant. Why?

Because God has scheduled both groups to be glorified together (Heb.11:39-40). The whole people of God, Old and New Covenant will be glorified together and enter their inheritance together (Rom.8:18-30). Those that are dead and those that are alive will all form one group (1Thess.4:13-18; 1Cor.15: 50-58).

In hope, the Patriarch Job speaks of this new world order when he said, "For I know that my Redeemer lives, and He shall stand at last upon the earth; and after my skin is destroyed, this I know, that in my flesh I shall God..." (Job 19:25-26 NKJV). By faith, Job sees himself in his glorified body standing upon the earth with the risen, ascended, glorified Redeemer who has returned to reign.

The people of God of the New Testament (covenant) also share the same vision of a new world order (Jer.31:31-37; Heb.8:7-13). It is strongly reflected in the promise of Jesus when He said, "I go to prepare a place for you, that where I am there, you may be also" (John 14: 1-4). Jesus is gone to prepare a place for His people; they are not a few, so it must be a place of some size, a city, or a planet. From what we now know, it is a new city (Rev.21-22).

A city is situated in a larger space. The ascended and glorified Christ revealed to the last of the apostles (i.e., John) that He is creating all things new, that includes a new heaven and a new earth (Rev.21:5). This brings us to the nature and content of the new creation or world order. The details are still classified but some things are revealed; we will look at some of the major things.

A New Heaven

Jesus said He is creating a new heaven (Rev.21:1). The first question people are likely to ask is—what and where is heaven? And the second--is the Jesus of the Bible able to do that? Let's consider the first question now and return to the second later.

The word heaven has at least two meanings: 1) it is a real place other than earth with the best quality of life, 2) it is a not a real place but a state of being, an experience of enjoyment and bliss. For example, the experience received from eating a delicious flavor of ice cream or attending a Broadway performance was so good, the people returning said, "It was out of this world; it was heavenly!" They are referring to the experience, the feeling, this fading otherness that they seek to memorialize.

Meaning #1 is the heaven of which we speak in this section; it is a real place with the best quality of life in all of creation.

The Word of God presents us with three levels of heaven. In fact, the Genesis creation record speaks of heaven in the plural. It says, "In the beginning God created the heavens and the earth" (Gen.1:1). We now know that there is a first, second, and third heaven.[1] We will briefly look at all three in this discussion.

The first heaven is called, the atmospheric heaven. The Bible speaks of the heaven where the birds fly and the clouds of heaven (Hos.2:18; Dan.7:13). And we speak of aircraft that fly through the heavens, above the clouds. The atmosphere extends above the earth higher than where the birds or aircrafts fly.

In fact, the atmosphere rises from the surface of the earth to about 6,200 miles (10,000 kilometers), that brings us to the very edge of space.[2] Scientists call this final level of the atmosphere, the exosphere. But there are four more levels before the exosphere; they are the troposphere, the stratosphere, the mesosphere, and the thermosphere.[3] All this together is the first heaven.

The second heaven is the planetary heaven (Gen.1:14-18). These heavenly bodies including sun, moon, and stars; these luminaries are also referred to as the hosts of heaven (Gen.2:1). The angels that fought on Israel's side in a battle are called stars or the heavenly hosts (Judges 5:20 NKJV). God is called, the LORD of hosts (Jer.5:14,38:17, 44:7; Hos.12:5 NKJV).

Some scholars believe that the second heaven is also the dwelling place for a vast number of angels of various ranks. They too are referred to as the heavenly hosts (Luke 2:13 KJV). Angels are at times referred to as stars (Rev.12:14). In fact, the name Lucifer means "day star" or "son of the morning;" he was one of .the bright luminaries of the heavens.

The third heaven is where God dwells (1Kings 8:27; Isa.6:1-7, 66:1; Rev.4:1-11). God, the Holy Trinity, does not dwell on this level alone, there are myriads of angels of high and other high-ranking beings here as well (e.g., cherubim, seraphim).

It is also evident that although angels dwell in the second heaven, they have frequent access to the third heaven (Job 1:6-9; Isa 14:12-15). It appears, therefore, that Lucifer's insurrection scheme was hatched at the second level but executed at the third level (Rev.12:7-9). Lucifer being an archangel had charge over many angels of varying ranks and tremendous access to God. It is like people travelling from various States to execute a takeover on the nation's capital, Washington D.C. They left their abode (Jude 6).

Furthermore, we have humans that were caught up to the third heaven. Enoch and Elijah were caught up to heaven (2 Kings 2:11; Heb.11: 5). The apostle Paul was taken to the third heaven (2 Cor.12:1-5). Jesus was taken up, and the apostle John as well (Acts 1:9-11; Rev.4:1-11). All this answers the first question that heaven is a real place away from earth. In as much as all the information says the where is up from earth, its exact location remains classified. We now turn to the second question.

Jesus said He is going to make all things new and that includes a new heaven, a real place away from earth. Building such a place is a massive undertaking. So, the second thing I would want to know is the builder's qualification to do such a project. Does He have any experience in heaven building? Can we see something He has built before? Even a fool would want to see evidence of a bridge builder's work before he is hired to construct such a critical structure.

We mortals are not hiring Jesus and we are not commissioning Him to build us a new heaven. Heaven building is a God thing. The Lord Jesus is a member of the Godhead, and the old creation we see is credited to him. The apostle John tells us, "He was with God in the beginning. Through him all things were made; without him nothing was made that was made" (John 1:2-3). The apostle Paul gives us further affirmation in the following quote.

> The Son is the image of the invisible God, the firstborn over all creation. For in him all things were created; things in heaven and on earth, visible and invisible, whether thrones or power or rulers or authorities; all things have been created through him and for him. He is before all things, and in him all things hold together. And he is the head of the body, the church; he is the beginning and the firstborn from among the dead, so that in everything he might have the supremacy (Col.1:15-18 NIV).

Yes, the Second Person of the blessed Holy Trinity is Jesus Christ and He is experienced in heaven building. He built the atmospheric heaven, and it has functioned well despite the damage humans have done to it. He created the planetary heavens and those bodies have stayed in their orbit, not causing any great problems to us here on earth. He also created the third heaven where God and millions of beings live and all have worked well, except for an attempted coup d'état, a rebellion that occurred with Lucifer and his followers. Well, the old heaven is old and was even desecrated by Lucifer's rebellion. That desecration was removed by the blood of Jesus (Heb. 9:23-26). If Lucifer left any fingerprints or desecration behind, it is no longer there. God creating a new dwelling place for Himself and His new family is a wonderful thing. The relocation of heaven closer to earth is in the new design. All this make great sense because there will be no more hostile forces to the kingdom of God.

What will be the contents of the new heaven? Much remain classified but the Word of God speaks about things of great value are in heaven. We know there are mansions (John 14:2 KJV). There are many crowns of gold (Rev.4:4, 19:12). Gold and precious stones are so plentiful, they are used to pave streets and as construction materials (Rev.21: 18-21). There are thrones in heaven, and at least one sanctuary or temple (Rev.4:2-6, 15:5-7).

Some scholars postulate that things on earth are copies of the true, original things in the heavenly realm (Ex.25:8-9;Heb.9:23-24). For example, the wilderness tabernacle and its furnishings, God instructed Moses to build it according to the pattern or plan shown to him on the mountain (Ex.25:40; Heb.8:5). The tree of life and the tree of knowledge that were in the Paradise Garden are all copies of the true things in heaven.

Since God is creating all things new, that implies that the new heaven will have new furnishings as well. The details remain classified. The King of creation has the best the universe has to offer; wealth is optimum, and this is wealth that is lasting.

But there is another kind of wealth that is not gold, silver, or precious stones that will be of greater value in heaven. They are love, justice and mercy, righteousness, kindness, forgiveness, goodness, honesty, faith, patience, hope—these are the currencies heaven values most. They are the treasures we are encouraged to store up in heaven; they have more lasting value (Matt.6:19-21).

We conclude the second question, therefore, that Jesus has the qualification to build a new heaven because He is God and the builder of the old heaven. But there is a third question.

If the Lord is making a new heaven, what will He do with the old one? This question seems almost trivial, but it is not. According to certain Bible passages, we could conclude that He is scrapping the old heaven. Revelation 20:11 tells us that "the earth and the heaven fled away," and there was found no place for them." Heaven and earth occupy space but here it says, no place was found for them. The implication is that they vanish into spaceless nothingness or from our reality. Vanish from reality? Yes, if they were spoken into existence by the Word of God, they can be spoken out of existence.

The apostle Peter tells us that the present heavens and earth were formed by the word of God, and "by the same word the present heavens and earth are reserved for fire, being kept for the day of judgment and destruction of the ungodly" (2 Peter 3:6-7). There you have it, that the present heavens will be destroyed, consistent with the apostle John assertion that it will vanish away (Rev.20:11). Peter in his continued discussion on the day of the Lord declares that "the heavens will disappear with a roar, and the elements will be destroyed by fire," melt with fervent heat (2 Peter 3: 10,12). This answers the third question about the old heaven. We turn our attention to the new earth.

A New Earth

Creation in total is the universe. The universe is a massive place with many systems, stars, and planets, including earth. The Lord said he would create all things new, and he specifies heaven and earth. Heaven is His dwelling and the seat of His government. Heaven is also the dwelling place of other beings as discussed earlier. Earth is His footstool, and the dwelling place of humans.[4]

Since humans are part of God's family and earth is our dwelling, God is putting us on notice that a new earth is also coming soon, and it may or may not have some of the things we have grown accustomed. It we take the Biblical text literally, "there will be no more sea" (Rev.21:1). But then again if the earth is going to vanish, it would vanish with the seas and the oceans.

The first thing the apostle John noticed about the new earth is that it has "no more sea" (Rev.21:1). What, no more sea! The context seems certain it is referring to sea of water. But it is hard for us to imagine earth without sea. For that reason, scholars have considered the different ways the word "sea" is used in scripture.

It is not always used in reference to water. For example, "And I saw a beast coming up out of the sea" (Rev.13:1-3). Here the beast is a man, and the sea is the mass of humanity or the wickedness of the present world. In Revelation (4:6), around the throne of God looks like a sea of glass. Even if there is no longer a gathering of waters called, sea, the new earth is not without rivers (Rev.22:1). In the gospels, the Sea of Galilee is a lake. When the new earth arrives, if indeed there is no more sea, we can nickname the River of Life, the Sea of Life. The sea issue is a small detail. R.C. Sproul asserts that sea was never a positive thing in the Hebraic mind.[5]

Scientists tell us this old earth is several billion years old. Obviously, it was well made; every time God added something to the earth, He said, it was good (Gen.1:3-31). God made the earth with vegetation, animals, seas, rivers, and the seasons. It is awe-inspiring, beautiful, functional, and life sustaining. But the Creator thinks it is time for a do over. May be the giraffe's neck might not be that long this time around; the Creator knows best.

But much of the things on old earth are man-made and are under the control of the evil one; Satan's fingerprints all over them. Human genius has made megalopolis, metropolis, entertainment centers, financial centers, educational institutions, and much more. To show that he controls all this, Satan once offered Jesus the kingdom of this world in all its sinful glory, if Jesus would worship him. Jesus refused his generous offer and run him off (Matt.4:8-11). The new earth will be most glorious; it will lack nothing.

A New Jerusalem

The old Jerusalem that King David made the capital city of Israel was the city of God; it was also called, Zion. It is where the Temple was, the place God put His name. Jesus will return to sit upon the throne of David and rule over the earth from this city (Isa.9:6-7). Jerusalem will remain the religious capital of Israel forever, not Tel Aviv.

Satan knows all that and has made a pre-emptive strike to stake his claim on Jerusalem, making it the city of controversy and bloodshed over the centuries. But despite Satan's clever move, he cannot prevent Jesus from returning to reign as Volumes 6 and 7 of this series have clearly established.

In the new world order, there will be two Jerusalem, the earthly and the heavenly (Rev.21-22). As already stated, the earthly Jerusalem is the renewed capital of Israel from which the Lord Jesus Christ will rule over the earth during His millennial reign. This earthly Jerusalem will remain the capital city of Israel forever. Even with the new earth, Jerusalem will remain Israel's capital city.

The Heavenly New Jerusalem is a massive city suspended over the earth, and accessible to the nations from all over the new earth (Rev.21:24). During the millennium, people from every nation will travel to the earthly Jerusalem to pay homage, at least once a year, to Jesus the King (Isa.60:1-22). The practice of traveling to Jerusalem was first a Hebrew thing up to A.D. 70 when the Romans destroyed it and the magnificent Herodian Temple. Perhaps a Third Temple will be built before or after Messiah arrive the second time.

But Jerusalem became a center Christianity also from Pentecost through the Middle Ages when Arabs fought and took it over. But despite that, Jerusalem to the 21st century never ceased being a place of pilgrimage. That pilgrimage will be required again of the kings of the nations during the Millennium.

But after the Millennium when the New Jerusalem comes down from God out of heaven and is suspended over the new earth, people will have access to it from all over the world without the need to travel to the earthly Jerusalem. The throne of the Lamb will be in the New Jerusalem with His Father's (Rev.22:3-5).

The apocalypse (the book of Revelation) speaks of the four corners of the earth as if it is a square; three of the twelve gates of the New Jerusalem is directed to one region of this four-directional earth. This makes it easy for the kings of the nations of the earth to access the capital, the New Jerusalem from their region (Rev.21:24). Furthermore, millions if not billions will dwell in New Jerusalem. And the new earth, perhaps, will accommodate more people than the old earth. The New Jerusalem is named for the Bride of Christ, the people of God (Rev.21 9-11).

Description of the New Jerusalem, the capital of the new earth. Earth never had a singular capital before.

- The New Jerusalem is a city of gold, built in heaven by heaven's architects and engineers; it is the city of God, the Holy City, the dwelling place of God, the seat of His Majesty's government over the universe (Rev.21:2-3).

- The city is about 1,400 miles square, with walls over 200 feet thick.[6] It has twelve foundations and twelve gates; each foundation is inscribed with the name of one of the twelve apostles of Christ. Each gate is made of a single pearl and is inscribed with the names of the twelve tribes of Israel. Three gates is on each of the four directions: East, West, North, and South (Rev.21:14-17).

- The foundations of the city are adorned with all kinds of precious stones: jasper, sapphire, chalcedony, emerald, sardonyx, sardius, chrysolite, beryl, topaz, chrysoprase, jacinth, and amethyst. "The street of the city [is] made of pure gold, like transparent glass" (Rev.21: 12-21).

The Glory of the City (Brightness, Splendor)

- The city has no natural light such as that of the sun or moon, but it is bright with the glory of God, sparkling as jasper stone, most precious, clear as crystal (Rev.21:10-11). The glory of God lights the city (vv.22-23). The apostle John tells us that "God is light and in him there is no darkness at all," and we can walk in the light of His countenance (1John 1:5-7). The face of Moses shone brightly after spending forty days and night in the presence of God (Ex.34:29-35). Jesus said, I am the light of the world. We now know He is not only the spiritual light or only the intellectual light of reason that gives every human ascendency over the brute creation (John 1:4-9). But He is the light in every sense of the word; the Lamb (Jesus Christ) is the light of the city (Rev.21: 23).

- The city has no building such as we would call a temple or sanctuary to meet God for worship, as we now do on the old earth. The whole city is the sanctuary, God Himself is the temple (v.22). The new creation will be filled with the glory of God as the waters now cover the sea. Worship is every activity, and it is continuous, not something done over there in a special building periodically.

- The New Jerusalem suspended over the new earth is the complete fulfillment of the prayer, "Thy kingdom come, thy will be done on earth at it is in heaven" (Matt.6:10 KJV). Heaven and earth will be connected as it has never been connected before. People from the four directions of the earth have three gates each to access heavenly city. God is still immortal but no longer invisible to us (Rev.22:3-4). We will be able to look upon His face because we too will be immortal (ICor.15:51-56).

- Because the glory of God that illuminates the city is constant, there will be no need for the sun or the moon, and there will be no night there. William Chatterton Dix (1860) in his classic hymn expresses it well: "In the heavenly country bright, need they no created light; Thou its light, its joy, its crown, Thou its sun which goes not down: There forever may we sing alleluias to our King."

- The twelve gates of the city are always open (Rev.21:25). This suggest freedom of movement and access without security concerns. Of course, all the bad guys are securely confined in their own place with no possibility of escaping (Rev.20:10,13-15).Despite all that there will be gate security (Rev.21:12). Check it out!

- The new world order includes, the new heaven, the new earth, and the new capital city, all reflect the character of God and His people: righteousness, holiness, truth, justice, and mercy (Rev.21:7-8, 27).

Summary

This chapter attempt to bring out of the Biblical text what has already been revealed about the new world order or creation to come. Many of the details are still classified, but our heavenly Father has slightly lifted the curtains and given us a glimpse of the awesome world of tomorrow. What is revealed is enough to keep us faithful, working in love until the curtains are fully lifted.

The world to come covers: the new heavens, the new earth, the New Jerusalem, or capital city, and much more. We have more information about the New Jerusalem than anything else.

The new creation will not have the deficits of the Fall that made the old creation a painful place of rebellion, war, violence, disease, and death; it will have no Satan roaming the earth making mischief. The old order of things are completely gone, even from our minds.

CHAPTER 3

THE PEOPLE OF THE NEW CREATION

Who are the people that will inherit and inhabit the new creation or live under the new world order? The entire Bible gives us insight who they are and who they are not. First, we will consider the negative, who will not inherit the kingdom of God and then who will. The only authoritative source to look to for the answers is the Word of God. The King of the kingdom has not left us in the dark on this matter.

The Word of God is not a set of suggestions; they are executive orders to be followed. They are directives from the Sovereign King of creation to His subjects and children to obey. The Word of God contains the character and will of God. Among humans, a man is no better than his words; if you cannot take him by his word, he is not trustworthy. God is not a man that He should lie; He is trustworthy.

We learn from our ancestral parents, the first children of God, that God is no respecter of persons; His words are agents of life and death. Life if they are obeyed and death if they are ignored. We read, "And the LORD God commanded the man, 'You are free to eat from any tree of the garden; but you must not eat of the tree of the knowledge of good and evil, for when you eat from it you will certainly die'" (Gen.2:16-17).

The key to eternal life lies in obedience to the Word of God. Humans are placed in the garden of earth with certain freedoms and certain restrictions. God has said to us in His Word, you are free to partake of many things I have created for your life. They are for your enjoyment, and human flourishing. But I am restricting you from a few things that will lead to your unhappiness and death; stay away from them and live! God's Word are guardrails of safety.

Rather than taking responsibility and obey the Word of God and live, we humans have the temerity and the audacity to ignore the Word of God, denying God of His freedom, then accuse Him of being unfair. People say, "Well if God knew that the tree with the poison fruits would have hurt Adam and Eve, He should not have put it in the garden." What are they doing when they say that?

They absolved the man and the woman of their responsibility to obey and restrict God of His freedom. This is the attitude that humans keep displaying through all of life, we try to play God. We have the same test as Adam and Eve, we obey the Word of God and live or we ignore it and die. We are creatures, not God!

The entire Bible is the Word of God. It is a library of 66 books, but in essence Jesus condensed its laws. The Law of Moses, the Torah has 613. Jesus condensed them to one, love for God and love for neighbor (your fellow humans). Additionally, God writes His law of love on our hearts and gives us the indwelling Holy Spirit to help us live it out in love (Jer.31:31-34; Heb.8:7-13; Matt.5:38-48).

In essence, the New Covenant, the Word of God is embodied in the person Jesus Christ (John 1:1-3, 14). Our relationship with Jesus Christ, enables us to obey God and live eternally. If we ignore Him, we die eternally (John 3:14-18). The people who want to be in the new creation, which is the kingdom of God, must follow these instructions given to us by the King Himself—you must be born again (John 3:1-6). Here is the key to the eternal city of God; it is offered to everyone here and now (i.e., while you are alive in the body). Ignore it and you die eternally; it is as simple as that.

Who Will Not Inherit the Kingdom of God?

The Word of God is very clear on this question. So, pay close attention now to what is being said in this section. Why? Because we have people dressed up in clerical vestments like me, calling themselves pastors, bishops, archbishops, cardinals, and popes talking out of two sides of their mouths in coded language. They dilute the Word of God and put your soul at risk.

They sugar-coat the Word of God, rather than telling you exactly what it says. They don't want to offend you, so they tell you exactly what you want to hear, rather than what you need to hear. They give you a false sense of security, which leaves you trying to be good, yet sitting in church on your way to hell without even knowing you are heading for hell (Matt.7:13-14). That is a false sense of security!

We are like our ancestral parents, Adam, and Eve, in paradise and got thrown out because they ignored the Word of God. We are doing the same thing; we ignore the Word of God. We think God loves us so much that we can live as we please and still gain entrance to the eternal city of God without repenting. That is a colossal mistake. Here are three lists of people that will not inherit the kingdom God; the Word of God has several, but we do three.

List #1: The person who is religious or unreligious and is not born again (John 3:1-5). This person could be devotedly religious or a complete unbeliever; he or she does not believe that Jesus is the Son of God, and that salvation comes through Him alone. If this person does not repent, he or she will perish (John 3:16-18). Read it for yourself; it is not written in hieroglyphics.

List #2: The words on this list are found in 1 Corinthians 6:9-10 (NKJV). "Do you not know that the unrighteous will not inherit the kingdom of God? Neither fornicators, nor idolators, nor adulterers, nor homosexuals, nor sodomites, nor thieves, nor covetous, nor drunkards, nor revilers, nor extortioners will inherit the kingdom of God." The list is not exhaustive; some things are on other lists.

This text of Scripture is abundantly clear that the people who go on practicing any of these sinful behaviors or lifestyles will not inherit the kingdom of God. No buts or ifs, no dancing around what is written will change this inspired, inerrant Word of God. But don't stop there. The next verse says, "And such were some of you. But you are washed, but you were sanctified, but you were justified in the name of the Lord Jesus, and by the Spirit of our God" (v.11).

The preceding verse means that God delivers from such abhorrent and sinful lifestyles that disqualify people from His Kingdom, but they must first repent. When a person truly repents, God sanctifies or cleans up that person in the blink of an eye. But it does not end there. God continues the cleansing work because sanctification is not only an event; it is a process. For example, when you bathe or take a shower, it is an event, but you do it again tomorrow or two days later. Thus, keeping clean is a process.

Look again at the verse, "And such were some of you. But you are washed, but you are sanctified, but you were justified in the name of our Lord Jesus Christ, and by the Spirit of our God" (1 Cor.6:11). Note that the words "washed" and "sanctified" come before the word "justified." Justify means God forgives us after we repent. He declares us righteous based on what Christ did on the cross. But He justifies us after He cleanses us. God will not justify what He cannot sanctify. You cannot be a "practicing" thief, murderer, adulterer, homosexual and inherit the kingdom of God.

It is a mockery of God and the sacrifice of Christ, to think we can ignore His Word and still inherit His kingdom. Jesus saves us from our sins, not in our sins (Matt.1:21). The Word of God is replete with warnings concerning those that will not enter or inherit the kingdom of God unless they repent and turn from their sins.

It appears hard and impossible, but you are not doing it alone. The Lord Jesus helps you; the Holy Spirit helps you to overcome that lifestyle. He delivers you from it. God's grace is sufficient.

List #3: Revelation 21:7-8 (NKJV). This list is given in the immediate context of the New Jerusalem. It says:

> He who overcomes shall inherit all things, and I will be his God and he shall My son. But the cowardly,

> unbelieving, abominable, murderers, sexually immoral, sorcerers, idolaters, and all liars will have their part in the lake which burns with fire and brimstone, which is the second death. (Rev.21:7-8 NKJV)

For emphasis, the persons in the preceding quotation are among the ones that will not inherit the kingdom of God, the list is repeated with some variations below:

> Blessed are those who do His commandments, that they may have the right to the tree of life, and may enter through the gates into the city. But outside are the dogs and sorcerers and the sexually immoral and murderers and idolaters, and whoever loves and practices lie. (Rev.22:14-15 NKJV)

These people are among those who will be shutout of the eternal city of God even though the gates are always opened.

We must therefore conclude that the Word of God is clear as to who will not inherit the Kingdom of God. The person who practices any of the lifestyles on the three lists identified and refuses to repent, will not inherit the kingdom of God. They are among the outsiders. What is the lesson here?

We must all examine ourselves against the Word of God to ensure we are truly born-again. Being born again is the only way we gain entrance to the kingdom of God (John 3:16-18). There is no other entrance or way provided in the Scriptures to eternal life.

Who Will Inherit the Kingdom?

The new creation, including the New Jerusalem, will be inherited by the people of God.[1] There is such a group of humans that the Bible refers to as the people of God. The apostle Peter declares:

> But you are a chosen people, a royal priesthood, a holy nation, God's special possession, that you may declare the praises of him who called you out of darkness into his wonderful light. Once you were not a people, but now you are the people of God; once you have not received mercy, but now you have received mercy. (1Peter 2:9-10).

Who are they? Again, the Word of God makes it abundantly clear who are the people of God. They are chosen from every nation, race, people, and culture around the world. In this section, we will zero in more closely on this group, citing several examples with their corresponding scripture passages.

First, the people of God are those people who have had a salvation relationship with Jesus Christ (John 3:14-18). They have entered the kingdom of God through a new birth experience (John 3:1-8). God transforms them by His redeeming grace (Rom.12:1-2).

Second, the people of God are book of life registrants (Rev.21: 27). This fact is emphasized again and again throughout the Bible, especially in the book of Revelation (13:8, 20:14-15). The Book of Life is the citizenship registry of the Kingdom of God.

Whatever nation we are born in on earth, we are registered and given a birth certificate to prove it. When we are born-again into the Kingdom of God, we are registered in heaven in the Lamb's book of life, and we are given the Holy Spirit (Heb.12:22-24; Eph.1:11-14). The Holy Spirit is the seal of God's ownership upon each believer in Christ, the down-payment of our heavenly inheritance (v.14). If a person does not have the Holy Spirit, he or she does not belong to Christ (Rom.8:9).

Third, Jesus speaks of those whom He will reward with an inheritance in His Kingdom in the Sermon on the Mount; He refers to them as the blessed ones (Matt.5-7). "Blessed are the poor in spirit, for theirs is the kingdom of heaven" (5:3). "Blessed are the meek, for they shall inherit the earth" (5:5). "Blessed are the peacemakers, for they shall be called sons of God" (5:9).

At the time this was spoken, sons were the ones in line to receive the inheritance from their fathers as the customs dictated. Most modern translation render the words "sons of God" as children of God. "Blessed are those who are persecuted for righteousness' sake, for theirs is the kingdom of heaven" (5:10).

Throughout the Sermon on the Mount and His subsequent ministry work, Jesus taught people how to be qualified to inherit the Kingdom of heaven. He invited them to a relationship of righteousness with Him, to make the kingdom of heaven and righteousness their priority (Matt.6:31-34).

Fourth, those who live a lifestyle of righteousness that exceeds that of the hypocritical scribes of Pharisees will enter the kingdom of heaven (Matt.5:20). In other words, a person's life must conform to the kingdom's lifestyle and culture now in this life. The local culture says, "Love your neighbor and hate your enemies," but kingdom culture says, "love your enemies, bless those who curse you, do good to those who spitefully use you and persecute you" (vv.43-45). The lifestyle of kingdom can only be lived with a relationship with Jesus Christ, which comes with the indwelling of the blessed Holy Spirit (Rom.8:9-10).

Fifth, Jesus gives another example of those who will inherit the kingdom and it is more than a relationship with Him; it includes how we treat people (Matt.25:31-46). In this passage, the Lord at His coming divides humankind into two groups: sheep and goats. The sheep on His right hand and the goats on His left. To those on his right the Lord said, "Come, you who are blessed by my Father, take your inheritance, the kingdom prepared for you since the creation of the of the world" (v.34). You ask, but on what basis?

On what basis do these people inherit the kingdom? The Lord said to them, "For I was hungry, and you gave me something to eat, I was thirsty, and you gave me something drink, I was a stranger and you invited me in, I needed clothes and you clothed me, I was sick and you looked after me, I was in prison and you came to see me" (vv.35-36). Their response to the Lord is, "when did we ever see you and did those things for you?" (vv.37-39).

The Lord responds, "whatever you did for one of the least of these brothers and sisters of mine, you did for me" (v.40). They were serving God by serving people in need; they had compassion for people and did not live selfishly.

But notice now those people on the Lord's left hand, the goat people. They had the same opportunity in life to serve people, but they did not. They chose to be uncaring, without compassion, and selfish. The Lord said to them, as much as you did not show kindness to the least of these my brothers, you did not do it unto me. He sentenced them to hell (vv.41-46).

A Glorified People

God says, "Behold, I make all things new;" He means "all," and He means "new" (Rev.21:5). It is a new world order with a new heaven, a new earth, a New Jerusalem, a new way of life, and a new people of God. But God has been calling out and shaping a new people all along to inherit the new heaven and the new earth.

First, the new world order will be occupied only by people who are redeemed. A new blood covenant was forged on Calvary and came into full effect with the resurrection of Jesus Christ from the dead (Jer.31:31-34; Heb.8:7-13). This covenant came with the new law of Christ written inwardly upon the hearts of people; it came with the indwelling Holy Spirit, making it possible to live victorious lives pleasing to God (Rom.8:3-10, 12:1-2).

The new covenant comes with a better sacrifice, a new priesthood, a better sanctuary, or temple (Heb.9:15,24-28). All this is to prepare a new people of God made up of both Jews and gentiles (Eph.2:4-22; 1Peter 2:9-10). They are also the new Temple.

God has been calling out and preparing a new creation people since Pentecost (Acts 2:1-4,14-41). Throughout the entire Church Age God has been calling out and preparing a new creation people for Himself. The apostle Paul declares, "Therefore, if anyone is in Christ, the new creation has come: The old has gone, the new is here!" (2 Cor.5:17).

Second, the new world order will be occupied only by people who are glorified. Glorification is the final stage of the believer's spiritual development (Rom.8:29). It is the perfection stage. The following are some characteristics of glorification:

- Glorified people are those who have been transformed or changed from corruptible flesh and blood to a state of incorruptibility and immortality. For this reason, the

righteous dead will be raised and are given new bodies suitable for the new world order living (1Cor.15: 42-44).
- Righteous human who have not experienced physical death will go through a process of transformation or change equivalent to physical death. It will happen in the blink of an eye (1Cor.15:50-54).
- The glorified children of God will inherit a glorified creation that is also "delivered from the bondage of corruption" (Rom.8: 18-21).

Third, there are things glorified people will no longer experience in the new creation. Here are a few of them: hate, jealousy, bloodshed, murder, lying, theft, and all that the Word of God had warned against. Such are old world behavior, consistent with the unredeemed life. There will be no more creation curse, no death, disease, sickness, sorrows, mourning, crying, poverty, and no Satan (Rev.20:10,13-14, 21:3-5).

What will New Creation People Do?

Let's ask the question again, what will new creation people be doing through eternity? The greater details of the new creation or new world order remain classified, not yet revealed to humans. But the little we do know from the Word of God is much.

The new creation will be magnificent, awe-inspiring! Frankly, there is no word invented yet to express the glory of the coming creation and city of God. We are going to need a new world vocabulary. We have never seen a city of gold before anywhere, shaped like a cube with twelve foundations; it is truly heavenly.

Yes, we are accustomed to massive passenger ships with several decks or floors, and people refer to them as floating cities. And we have seen skyscrapers of awe-inspiring size and grandeur with many floors. But human eyes have not beheld any earthly city of such magnificence as the New Jerusalem; it is indeed out of this world, yet on its way coming down to us (Rev.21:2).

The fact that God is relocating to dwell with humans (v.3), may hold a clue as to what we will be doing. For sure we will not be clad in white robes, floating around on white clouds playing harps; that's a product of a fictional imagination. Let's decode the clue of God relocating His dwelling and universal administrative center to dwell with humans, His new, glorified family.

First, God has a work ethic; the Bible opens with God at work creating the old creation. He created man, gave him a job to work a garden, and assigned the race to manage the earth (Gen.1:26-28, 2:8,15; Ps.8:3-9). God created humans with a work ethic; the entire written word of God abhors, idleness and laziness (Prov.6:6-11).

God rested on the seventh day, but He did not go on vacation. Jesus said, "My Father is always at his work this very day, and I too am working" (John 5:17 NIV). God is providentially managing His creation (Matt.6:25-31). It is interesting that the Bible ends with God showing up with a new heaven, a new earth, and a new city he has been building all this time. We should have known because Jesus said He was leaving to prepare a place for us in His Father's house (John 14:1-3). Heaven is God's house, His dwelling place.

Second, although church folks preach and sing about going to heaven, our trip to old heaven will be a short visit for about seven years as discussed in Volumes 1 and 3. We will be in heaven during the length of the Great Tribulation on a working vacation, and we will return to earth at the end of the tribulation (Rev.19:11-15).

Heaven will be coming closer to earth. To the righteous, wherever Jesus is personally present is heaven. The Word of God informs us that Jesus is coming to reign (Isa.9:6-7; 1Cor.15:25; Rev.21:1-7). It also reveals that His people will not only inherit the earth, but they will also reign on and over the earth as kings, lords, and priests with Jesus (Matt.5:5; 2Tim.2:12, Rev. 21:7). The people of God will reign upon the earth (Rev.5:9).

Additionally, the following seems clear from the Word of God:

- God is moving His dwelling (the third heaven) closer to earth. His dwelling includes His universal administrative center, which is the capital city, the New Jerusalem (Rev.21:1-2).

- God's purpose for relocating is to dwell with His new family (vv.3-7). His family is glorified humans; they will reign with the Father and the Son and manage the earth and universe with them (Heb.1:1-8). It was God's purpose from the beginning to dwell with humans as we have seen with Adam and Eve in the Paradise Garden. God partners with humans in both creation and redemption, but sin disrupt that relationship. The new world order is the perfection of what God was after form the beginning. God has now fully reconciled Himself to humans; they are His family.

- Glorified humans will be kings and priest among other leadership titles. God will be managing the universe from His new dwelling and headquarters, and humans will be key managers in this new world order.

- Will other worlds and planets be populated by other beings? If so, will the family of God have management responsibility over them? Such information is not yet revealed; it is classified. The possibilities are endless, but we have eternity to explore them all.

Summary

So, what will humans be doing in the new world order? We will be working. Glorified human beings will not be sitting on thrones with crowns on their heads picking their nails and doing nothing. The very thought of that is absurd! God has not surrendered His work ethic, and neither will we. God is always at work.

We have a universe to manage. Work will not be unpleasant and laborious as it was in old creation. It was like that because of sin and the curse but the former things are done away with.

Knowing Jesus as Savior and Lord is fundamental to entering the kingdom of God. Being a citizen of the kingdom of God is more than being baptized in water and becoming a member of a local church. It is having a life transforming relationship with Jesus Christ, a new birth experience (John 3:1-18; Rom.12:1-2; 2Cor.5:17).

Your relationship with Jesus Christ must move you to serve Him and neighbor out of love and compassion. You serve God by serving people. All that we do now in the kingdom is rehearsal for the perfect world to come, a world over which we will be given ownership and management.

CHAPTER 4

ANGELS AND THE NEW WORLD ORDER

Overview

Humans and angels are not in the same class of beings now and there is no scriptural evidence that the distinction will change in the new world order. We will briefly explore what we know about these powerful and important beings in the Kingdom of God.

We know angels are created beings (Col.1:15-16). They were created before the creation of the world because they were present in joyful celebration when God completed His creation work. We are told in Word of God that the morning stars shouted for joy (Job 38:6-7). The implication is that they were here before, but how long before, we do not know. Like humans, they were created holy and given responsibilities (Jude 6). But Human beings were "created a little lower than the angels" (Ps.8:5). But what does the expression "a little lower than" mean? It could mean several things.

First, it could mean humans are positionally lower than angels. We were made of dust to dwell upon the earth. Whereas angels were made of something else that does not age, get sick or die, and they dwell in the second heaven with access to the third heaven as well as the earth. They are not limited by gravity to one planet.

Second, lower may mean humans are created weaker and with lesser capabilities than angels. Angels are bigger and stronger than humans; they have greater capabilities. One angel slay one hundred and eighty-five thousand troops in one night (2Kings 19:35).

Third, lower may simply mean that humans are a different class of beings, not inferior, just different, unique, and special. And indeed, we are! because humans are created in the image and likeness of the Creator Himself and are crowned with glory and honor and are given charge over God's earth (Gen.1:26; Ps. 8:1-9).

Fourth, humans have a coveted relationship status with God. We are sons and daughters, heirs of God and co-heirs with His only begotten Son Jesus Christ; we are family (John 1:12; Rom.8:15-17).

Fifth, God became human in the person of Jesus Christ to redeem the humans after they failed (John 1:1-5,14). Like humans, angels were created holy; they also failed (not all), but unlike humans, angels were not given redemption (Heb.2:10-11).

Sixth, angels are very powerful beings, superior in strength to humans. They are in various ranks or classes such as regular angel, archangel, cherubim, seraphim, and the like. They are in the service of God's government, and they all worship (Isa.6:1-3; Rev.5:11-12).

Seventh, unlike humans, angels are not sexual beings; they do not get married or procreate (Matt.22:30). In this sense glorified humans will be like angels, but they will not be angels.

Some angels might have been sexual in the distant past and procreated with the daughters of men and produced a class of giants known as Nephilim (Gen.6:1-8). There is a controversy as to who were the "sons of God" (v.2). Their offsprings were giants (v. 4). The theory that "the sons of God" were angels who cohabitated with the daughters' men to produce a race of giant, postulates that was the wickedness that precipitated Noah's flood (vv. 4-5).

Another theory is that "the sons of God" were the descendants of Seth, the third son Adam. He represents the godly line because in his time people began calling upon the name of the Lord again (Gen.4:25-26). There are scripture passages that identify "the sons of God" to be angels (Job 1:6,2:1,38:7). But it is possible that "the sons of God" in the Genesis passage were not angels, because Jesus informs us that the angels are not sexual beings (Matt.22:30). Perhaps that should end the controversy right there.

We do know that some angels are so bad, they are not allowed to roam the earth with Satan and his demons to do mischief. Instead, they are kept in maximum security prisons in chains under darkness waiting for the day of judgment (2Peter 2:4; Jude 6). They will be judged and thrown into hell with Satan(Rev.20:1-3,7-12). We have no idea what is the nature of their wickedness that set them apart from Lucifer who has some freedom of movement.

The Present Work of Angels

First, like humans, angels of all ranks are worshipping beings; they worship God, and they do it very well (Isa.6:1-6; Rev.4, 5). Humans are forbidden to worship angels; it is an act of idolatry to worship anything and anyone other than God (Ex.20:3-7; Deu.6:4-5). Angels are quick to tell humans who assume a posture of worship in their presence not to do that (Rev.22:8-9).

Second, everything in creation is under God's administration and for the most part falls under one angelic portfolio or another. God runs an orderly universe and angels are given responsibilities over different systems in the natural world. Some are guardian angels that minister to the people of God (Heb.1:13-14). Small children, particularly have a special class of angels that report directly to God on their behalf (Matt.18:10; Mark 1:13-16). This signals that the welfare of children is top priority to God.

Third, there are territorial angels that stand guard over certain nations and regions of the world. The archangel Michael, we know stands guard over Israel. Satan does the same thing with his angels, but where did he get that idea from? Satan structures his kingdom off the kingdom of God because that is what he knows.

Fourth, the atmosphere, the weather, wind, fire, rain, storm, vegetation--their activity can be explained scientifically, because there are certain natural laws that govern their consistency. But they are also under the ministry of angels who regulate them to the glory of God. They are God's agents everywhere in His creation. God is intimately involved in His creation. Nature can be released as an act of divine judgment as was Noah's flood and the destruction of Sadom and Gomorrah (Gen.7:1-12,19:23-25; 2 Peter 2: 4-6).

Fifth, there are angels that administer justice and execute judgments like law enforcement and military officers do in a human context. These angels execute orders, but they do not make judicial decisions, such as a court would render, that is left to the Godhead, and most often to the Son of God. For example, the *Lucifer Uprising* in heaven was quickly put down by militant angels led by Archangel Michael (Rev.12:7-9). When an angelic envoy sent to the prophet Daniel, was detained by one of Satan's strong angels, Michael, the archangel was summoned to help (Dan.10: 12-14).

When King David yielded to Satan's temptation to number Israel, God made the decision to punish David, but that punishment was carried out by a destroying angel who received his order from God from start to finish (1 Chron.21:1-30). Judgment upon Saul of Tarsus, and Ananias and Sapphira was salvation related and was executed by the Son and the Holy Spirit, not angels (Acts 5,9).

Sixth, the assignment of some angels is to bring information to humans; they are envoys. Even though the word angel means messenger, not all ranking angels have that assignment. In both the Old and New Testaments, we frequently see Gabriel on messenger assignment (Dan.8:16, 9:21; Luke 1:19, 26-38).[1]

Seven, there are other angels that appear to be guardians of God's glory; they are called Seraphim and Cherubim; sometimes referred to as living creatures. They are always around the throne of God, even carrying it (Isa.6:1-7;Ezek.1 5-28;Rev.4 6-10).

The Work of Angels in the New World Order

The study of angels is called angelology, that's not what we are trying to do in this chapter, because angelology is a very extensive study that would require a whole book or series of books. We are just trying to gain insight as to how these mighty beings worked in the past, how they function now in the kingdom, and what their assignments will be in the new world order in relations to glorified human beings. We want to stay close to the biblical text as possible.

Frankly, we have no scriptural evidence that the function of angels will be any different from what they are now. Perhaps, their assignment to humans will be slightly adjusted, since humans will be glorified and not need all that babysitting as before.

In our state of glorification, we will have greater capabilities close to that of the angels if not surpassing them. Of course, humans will not be angels, but we will be like them in at least one area; we will no longer procreate (Matt.22:29-30).

We will also be able to move seamlessly between the new heaven and the new earth without the restriction of gravity. This will be possible because we will have glorified bodies like that of our Lord Jesus Christ (Acts 1:9-11;1Thes.4:16-17; Phil.3:20-21).

Angels will be very busy during the countdown from the time of the rapture to the establishment of the new world order. Their activities during that time provide us with insight and a better understanding into the angels' continued function in the service of the Almighty in the new world order.

First, note that angels will accompany Jesus when he calls for His people at the rapture. The Bible tells us that "the Lord himself shall come down from heaven with a loud command, with the voice of the archangel and with the trumpet call of God, and the dead in Christ will rise first" (1 Thess.4:16).

Second, the wrath of the Lamb (Jesus Christ) during the seven years of Great Tribulation will be largely administered by angels:

- The four horsemen of the apocalypse (Rev.6).
- The sealing of the 144 thousand (Rev.7:1-8).
- The trumpet judgments (Rev.8).

- The angel given the key of the bottomless pit(Rev.9).
- The angel with the little scroll (Rev.10).
- The three angels with everlasting gospel (Rev.16 6-13).
- The angels give the sharp sickle to reap the earth (Rev.14:14-20).
- The seven angels with the seven last plagues (Rev.15-16).
- The mighty angel announcing the fall of Babylon (Rev.18).
- An army of saints and angels that accompany Jesus on His return to earth (Rev.19:11-16).
- The angel call the birds of prey to the great supper (Rev.19:17-18).

Third, Satan a fallen angel is arrested by a mighty angel of light, chained, and thrown into the bottomless prison for a thousand years (Rev.20:1-3). He does seem all that that powerful now, does he? The old boy in placed in custody; his freedom taken away.[2]

Fourth, angels are reapers at the end of the age; they are the ones rounding up people for judgment (Matt.13:39; 25:).

Fifth, it was an angel who introduced the New Jerusalem, the heavenly city of gold, to the apostle John (Rev.21:9-26).

Sixth, it is an angel that introduced the apostle John to the River of the water of life (Rev.22:1-5).

Summary

The apostle John who gives us the book of Revelation is the last of the apostles to have died; he speaks as the representative of the Church age in this book. The revelation given to him by the risen, glorified, ascended, exalted Christ, unveils the course of history to the new world order. He shows us what will happen to the people of God, the wicked, Satan, and old created order.

The glory of the exalted Christ clearly knocked John off his feet when John first saw him (Rev.1:10-19). The flesh and blood apostle could not stand the intensity of divine glory. The vision was later mediated to him by an angel who exerts less intensity (Rev.1:1).

John was caught up to heaven in chapter four (Rev.4:4). And he is under angelic escort through heaven as the contents of the book are unveiled to him to the end. He saw worship going on in the throne room of God; he saw Jesus the Lamb of God at work in heaven (Rev.4-6). He the rise of the Antichrist and his sidekick the False prophet (Rev.13). John witnessed the administration of judgment by the Lamb through the Great Tribulation period, the coronation and marriage supper of the Lamb, and His return to earth to triumph over the Antichrist and Satan and to reign (Rev.19).

The last few things shown to the apostle John by his escorting angel or angels is the new world order with the New Jerusalem, the river of the water of life, and the tree of life (Rev.21:9-26; 22:1-5).

What will the angels be doing in the new world order? It appears they will be doing what they now do with some adjustment. They will not need to babysit humans because humans will be in their glorified state and more like Jesus (1John 3:1-3). Furthermore, all enemies of Christ and His people, including Satan, would be vanquished from the creation. The angels are likely to have some adjustment in their assignments on the minus side and on the plus side. The angels, therefore, will be very much busy serving God in the new world order as they do now. Anything else is classified for now.

CHAPTER 5

THE GOVERNMENT OF THE NEW WORLD ORDER

The concepts of family, nation, and government find their origin in God; He is the original architect (Gen.1:26-28, 2:18-25). It is instructive that in the book of beginnings, God laid the foundation for the three most important institutions upon the earth: the family, the nation, and government. God emphasized His intention to Noah, Abraham, Moses concerning government and growing families into nations (Gen.9:4-7,12:1-2, 17:1-8).

God gives human government the power to protect the sanctity of life, and the authority to demand the life of the murderer as just punishment for any human life taken with malice (Gen.9:5-6; Ex.20:13;). The murderer is not guiltless; his life is demanded for the life he takes, because each human is the image bearer of God. The sanctity of human life must be understood in the context of power and justice. God by nature is all powerful and just, for that reason He restrains Himself by mercy in the administration of justice towards humans who are weaker beings. For that same reason, God requires justice and mercy in human relationships (Micah 6:8). Because He is just and merciful by nature, God deals with murder differently to manslaughter. One is by premeditation and malice or intent to do harm, while the other is by accident.

It is against this background, God directed Moses to establish cities of refuge where the person who accidently slay or kill a person could flee for protection until proper investigation could be made (Ex.21:12-13). At first the sanctuary was where the killer could run for safety. But if it is found that the accused did the killing by premeditation, he would be removed from this safe place and executed for his crime (v.14). The same was true for the cities of refuge; the guilty could not hide out there as a fugitive from justice.

If the killing proved to be accidental, he remains in the safe place until the High Priest dies, then he was free to return home. But if proven guilty, he would be taken from his safe place and be executed. Six Cities of Refuge were established throughout ancient Israel for this purpose (Jos.20:1-6).

Even in our time there are cities in the United States that are designated as sanctuary cities, but their functions are somewhat different because of a more advanced judicial system. The point is that God created human governments and entrusted them with the sword to protect the sanctity of human life and administer justice

(Rom.13:1-7). These ideas of justice that that are now commonplace in Western jurisprudence are all traceable to God Himself, the authentic giver of life and are documented in the Torah.

The ancient nation of Israel was God's model of the nation He wanted. God's intent from the very beginning was to create a people in His image and likeness as an extension of His family. His purpose was to dwell among them as demonstrated in the Paradise Garden where God came down to fellowship with humans on earth, but the fellowship was broken by reason of the Fall (Gen.3:8-12).

God's purpose is family building, and nation building, so that He could dwell with humans; that means bringing the culture of heaven to earth, thus the familiar biblical saying, "Thy kingdom come, thy will be done on earth as it is in heaven" (Matt.6:10 KJV). From the beginning then, God's purpose is to replicate the culture of heaven on earth with humans as His agents and family.

The Tower of Bable fiasco was Satan's attempt to frustrate the purpose of God from populating the whole earth for nation building (Gen.11:1-9). Many are the plans in a man's heart, even Satan, but it is the purpose of God that prevails. Despite the Babel tower builders' valiant effort, God scattered them over the face of the earth to achieve His purpose of many families and many nations.

Satan has not abandoned his plan to frustrate God's purpose; he is persistently at it night and day. And from the Garden of Eden, he has been recruiting human beings to do his bidding. People have numerous ways of corrupting themselves to detract from the ways of God. The prophet Isaiah unveils to us God's mind in this regard when he said, "For my thoughts are not your thoughts, neither are your ways my ways declares the Lord" (Isa.55:8). Since the Fall in Paradise, humans have been going their own way (53:6).

God started over to build a godly family from which He would build a godly nation as a model for the whole world. This we see with the call of Abraham and the shaping of Israel. But again, Satan stepped it to corrupt and hinder Israel throughout its history from God's best. Satan may be the cause for putting God's plan on detour, but Satan can never succeed in aborting it; the purpose of God will always prevail (Isa.55:8-11).

From the golden calf to the Israel's exile to Assyria, and Judah's exile to Babylon, from Roman occupation to Hitler's holocaust and Hamas' terrorism in 2023, Satan has been working to destroy Israel. Satan provokes Israel to us terror in response to terror. In so doing he is using both sides to do his bidding. How does a nation respond to terror without using terror themselves? This is a question for the expert. Satan's effort is to stir up worldwide hate against Israel; Israel, therefore, must respond to terror with resolve and godly wisdom. Perhaps taking the higher moral road.

Satan recruits, sometimes, one person or one family at a time. He is repulsed that God has chosen a people to dwell among be it Israel, the Church or both; his mission is to destroy (Rev.12:1-17).

From the early history of Israel, God made it clear that He was calling out a people to Himself, and He would dwell among them. They would be a nation of priests, His special treasure to Him, and they would be the conduit through which He blesses all nations upon the earth. So, God said to Moses build me a sanctuary that I might dwell among them (Gen.12:1-3; Ex.19:5-6). But again, the evil one stepped into the equation to frustrate the plan of God.

Adam was crowned as king over the earth under God, and Eve Adam's consort (Gen.1:26-28; Psalm 8:1-8). Satan stepped into Eden and corrupted the family, and that effort of Satan continues to the present time. The family has been under relentless attack by the evil one; he wants to destroy God's model. Satan is working on two fronts; the first is to destroy God's model for the family, and two, to destroy God's model for the nations. He started on both from Eden. The 21st century has seen emerged a model of family that is antibiblical, and the Church seem powerless in its wake.

A nation is a large group of families, each family is the basic building block of the nation. Satan's plan to destroy God's plan for Israel can be traced back to the Pharaoh that made them slaves. But God's purpose for the family and the nation remains the same.

God's Preferred Form of Government

God's preferred for a government is theocracy as reflected in His early relationship with the nation Israel. I am not speaking of so-called Medieval or modern-day theocracy that want to live flourishing lives while embracing the "eye for an eye, tooth for a tooth" philosophy rather than the "love thy neighbor as thy self.

For theocracy to truly work, the sovereign must be the God of the Bible, and humans must be spiritually changed from within. Jesus refused to restore the David kingdom to Israel without a spiritual transformation from within. That is what Jesus offered His own people under the new covenant, but they rejected it.

God can work with just about any form of government, but it must the moral law as reflected of the Ten Commandments and the Sermon on the Mount. Only people with new a transforming experience of redeeming grace can truly live out God's moral law.

God was not pleased when Israel exchanged theocracy for monarchy during the time of Samuel, the prophet (1 Sam.8 4-9). Yet, Israel's golden years were under Kings David and Solomon.

They were not perfect kings, but they did not seek to evict God from the national life. God was able to dwell among His people. So, God can work with a government that is not theocratic in form.

But He will not work with any government that cast righteousness, truth and justice to the wind and expect to flourish. It is true that "righteousness exalts a nation, but sin is a disgrace to any people" (Prov.14:34). When Israel persistently went after other gods, the glory of God departed from them and were eventually driven off their covenant land. All this happened because they were not spiritually changed from within.

God promised to make a new covenant with the house of Israel and the house of Judeah. This time God would write His law upon their hearts and give them the Holy Spirit to enable them to live righteously (Jer.31:31-37). This new covenant came into being with the Messiah, Jesus Christ. Israel wanted Jesus to restore the Davidic kingdom, but they rejected God ruling over them from the heart through Jesus Christ. They denounced Jesus Christ and moved the Roman governor to execute Him.

Israel rejected Jesus Christ and that wholesale rejection caused the delay of restoration of the David kingdom. Why? They could not be able to keep the land if they were not wont inwardly. It is that spiritual failure that caused the exile to Assyria and Babylon, and the Roman occupation. They were uncircumcised inf their hearts. Jesus prophesied that they would be driven off the land and their place of worship destroyed (Matt.24:1-8). The Romans fulfilled this prophecy of the destruction of the Temple in A.D. 70.

Throughout the Church age, God has been calling out a people for Himself, a people who is won inwardly, both Jews and Gentiles (Rom.10:10-13). And Israel must be won inwardly to Yeshua by the

Holy Spirit to enjoy David's kingdom when it is restored on the second advent of the Messiah. The world is moving back to God's preferred form of government, a theocracy. The millennial reign of Jesus Christ upon the throne of David is the full restoration of the Davidic Kingdom to Israel (Isa.9:6-7). That is theocracy restored for a thousand years (see Volumes 6 and 7).

An Everlasting Theocracy

After the millennium, the world will not revert to any previous form of government. The old order of things will be destroyed and there will be a new heaven, a new earth, and a new capital called, the New Jerusalem, suspended in what used to be the atmospheric heaven over the new earth. The dwelling place of God will be redesigned, made visible, and moved much closer to earth. In fact, it is almost made one with the new earth.

All this comes into play after the final judgment when the wicked humankind, Satan, demons, fallen angels, and the works of mankind are swept away from the creation forever. The God-Man, Jesus Christ has defeated and vanquished all enemies, and has now handed over the reins of government to the Father (1 Cor.15). From here on the Father and the Son rule jointly forever (Rev.21:1-4).

The details of the new world order are classified. But the following appears to be the structure:

- The seat of government where the Godhead resides is in the New Jerusalem that is suspended over the new earth. It has an open-gate policy, but angelic guards are posted (Rev.21:12).

- There will be no Temple or sanctuary or megachurch building in the city (Rev.21:22). The whole city will be the sanctuary with the throne of God at the center of worship.

- The human Kings/Priests that rule over the nations on the new earth will bring their glory into the New Jerusalem (Rev.21:24). They will all have freedom access from their region of the new earth to the New Jerusalen.

- Israel will remain as a nation with the earthly Jerusalem its new capital, not Tel Aviv.

Few Outstanding Features of the New Jerusalem.

The River of the Water of Life is one of the outstanding features of the New Jerusalem; it flows directly from the throne of God down main street of the great city (Rev.22:1-2). It is spectacular and awe-inspiring. The escorting angel showed this river to the apostle John.

Presently, everything on earth is related to something in the spiritual realm that is said to be more real than its earthly counterpart. Life on earth is impossible without water. The present earth is largely made up of water, and every living thing needs water to live. Not so in the new world order; life will not be dependent on water as we know it in the old world. Perhaps that is why we are told first that there will be no more sea (Rev.21:1).

The life of the human body is in the liquid called blood. But note that the life-principle of our new body will not be blood. Flesh and blood cannot inherit the kingdom of God (1 Cor.15:50-57). The physical body in under the sentence of death and must be changed and become glorified to enter the kingdom of God permanently. This process of change begins with the new birth (John 3:1-8, 16).

Jesus in His post-resurrection body said, a spirit does not have flesh and bone as you see me have (Luke 24:36-43). Note that blood is conspicuously absent. Jesus was now in His spiritual or glorified body. The life-principle of the glorified body is in the spirit not blood. Our glorified body will be real as the resurrection body of Jesus (1John 3:3). It will not be subject to the former limitations.

Jesus said, "I am the water of life" (John7:37-39). What does that mean? The expression "water of life" or "living water" was used by Jesus symbolically as a reference to salvation or eternal life in Christ (John 4:4-14). Just as natural water is a life source for the physical body, Jesus is the life source for our spiritual existence. But *the River of the water of life* that flows through the New Jerusalem is all that and more. It appears to be a real river that imparts life-sustaining energy. Water is a life source, but water is also a very destructive force, but not here in the New Jerusalem. It can only add life to life as we move from glory to glory in Jesus Christ.

The tree of life is a second feature of interest here in the New Jerusalem. The Word of God says, "On each side of the river stood the tree of life, bearing twelve crops of fruits, yielding its fruit every month. And the leaves of the tree are for the healing of the nations" (Rev.22:2 NIV). Have you noted the three peculiar things about the tree of life: 1) It is on each side of the river, 2) it gives a crop of fruits each month, 3) the leaves are for the healing of the nations. There will be no sickness, disease, or death anymore. So, healing signifies something we don't quite understand at this time.

The tree of life first appears in the *Garden of Eden*, in the very middle of the garden (Gen.2:9). Before Adam and Eve sinned, they had access to the tree of life, but we do not know for sure if they ate from it. After they sinned, they were expelled from the garden and bared from the tree of life. But here in the closing chapters of the Bible Eden is restored with the tree of life occupying a central location again (Rev.22:1-5). Indeed, Paradise is fully regained.

The creation including earth will become the perfect utopia, more perfect than the millennium. There were rebels living during the millennium and Satan used them as his attacking army against Christ and His people. He promptly assembles this army upon his release from prison (Rev.20:7-10). Not so with the new world order, Satan and his rebels and all evil are forever gone form the creation. The environment will be perfect; there will be no more curse (Rev.22:3). A world without Satan; a world without evil, and without sinful human nature will be heaven on earth indeed.

The Throne of God and the Lamb is the supreme feature of the New Jerusalem. Here is the KING of the universe: Father, Son, and Holy Spirit. This is the seat of universal government. The invisible God becomes visible, His light no longer inaccessible from our eyes; His people will now look upon His face, live, and walk in the light of His countenance, because we are in our glorified state (Rev.22:4).

The nations of the earth will be ruled over by representative Kings and Priests as part of the theocratic government structure. The form of theocratic structure of the millennium, appears to continue in the new world order with some minor adjustments.

In the millennium Christ rules from the earthly Jerusalem as KING of Kings and LORD of Lords. He returns to earth with that title and with many crowns on His head (Rev.19:1-16). This means He does not return to rule alone. Glorified saints that were raptured to heaven and awarded crowns return to earth to rule with Him. But now He is not on David's throne in earthly Jerusalem, but the New Jerusalem on His Father's throne ruling jointly (Reev.22:3-4).

The nations that are given the right of passage to enter the millennium after the Judgment of nations are ruled over by regent kings who are responsible to the Chief KING in earthly Jerusalem. The nations are no longer making pilgrimage to the earthly Jerusalem but the new where the KING sits on His throne.

So, nations will still be upon the new earth more glorious than they have ever been, and they are ruled over by kings and priests under the main theocracy in the New Jerusalem. These nations will bring their glory into the capital city from different regions of the earth all year round (Rev.21 24-26). That is one of the reasons the gates to the New Jerusalem will always be opened; that suggests ease of access to the Father's house.

New Jerusalem Worship

The New Jerusalem holds the constancy and centrality of worship. All persons in the new creation with be in a glorified state; our understanding and capacity for worship will be greatly expanded if not limitless. We will not become tired, weary, or fatigued worshipping as we do now in a physical body. Our new, glorified bodies are designed for the intensity of the divine presence and worship experience. Worship will not be periodic, but as natural and constant as breathing was in our previous old earth body.

Every action now is an act of worship, so worship will be constant. The object of all activity is God and the Lamb; for that reason, the entire New Jerusalem will be the sanctuary. No one building is set apart as the Temple. Each person is the temple of God and collectively the entire City of God is the Temple of God.

During the Church Age each believer is the temple of God, and all believers together constitute the Temple of God as well

(1Cor.6:19-20; Eph.2:11-22). In like manner, in the new world order, each child of God remains a temple or a spiritual stone in God Temple as the apostle Peter noted (1Pet.2:4-9). But the entire new Jerusalem is the Temple of God, the wife of the Lamb, the general assembly and Church of the first born (Heb.12:22-24; Rev.21: 1-4, 9-14). All dwellers of the City of God, at least, will be glorified saints.

The New Jerusalem is the dwelling place of God and the Lamb, so what we see in the biblical text is the centrality and constancy of worship (Rev.21-22). Worship is at the heart of this theocratic government. The old heaven also had the centrality and constancy of worship (Rev.4-5); the new heaven retains this feature.

But worship is not confined just to the Capital City, the whole new creation is worshiping God because the cursed that was placed on creation is no more (Rev.22:3). Every nation on the new earth will have their capital city where worship is central and constant. All capital cities are ruled by Regent Kings and Priests are connected to the New Jerusalem with frequent orderly access.

The kings and priests of the new earth which are all glorified leaders will bring their glory from all the nations to the capital city, the New Jerusalem throughout the year (Rev.21:24-26). That is one reason the twelve gates of the New Jerusalem are never closed.

If people were not going and coming, there would be no need for gates. Gates are both entrances and exits. As we say in New York, this is the city that never sleeps. The twelve gates of the eternal city are always open, but make no mistake there are angelic guards at each gate (Rev.21:12). Because our God is One of protocol and order (1 Cor.14:33). The worship of God will always be awe-inspiring, enthusiastic, dynamic (Isa.6:1-4; Rev.4:1-11, 19:1-8).

Another thing to bear in mind is this—the New Jerusalem is the Universal Capital, not just the capital of earth; it will be closer and visible to earth, yes. But if the other planets in the universe are brought to life with other beings, the New Jerusalem where God resides is the capital city over them all, the administration center.

We humans are earth dwellers, so our focus now is the earth and our relationship to the New Jerusalem. But the universe is not just made up of earth; God's rule extends far beyond earth. He rules over the whole creation. And remember, much of what we will know in heaven remains classified until we get there, or heaven comes to us (1 Cor.13:12).

Summary

We set out to look at the form of government that will be over the new world order. We find that from the time of ancient Israel, God's preferred form of government is theocracy. It is a government over which God Himself is the Supreme ruler; that preference has not changed. How do we know that?

The millennium is a demonstration of theocracy at work. Jesus returns to earth with many crowns on His head and the title KING of Kings and LORD of Lords written across His vestment (Rev.19:16).

He is King and Priest and He is God. He comes to fulfill the prophecy that says, "...and the government shall be upon his shoulders. And he will be called Wonderful Counselor, Mighty God, Everlasting Father, Prince of Peace..." (Isa.9:6-7).

But He does not return to rule alone; those awarded with crowns at the *Believers' Judgment* will rule upon the earth with and under His supervision. During the millennium, Christ rules from the earthly Jerusalem, the seat of His government, sitting on the throne of David, (Isa.9:7). It is partial answer to the prayer, let "thy kingdom come." The new world order is the full coming of the Kingdom.

At the end of the millennium Satan and all enemies and evil will be fully vanquished from God's creation, and the old order will be completely destroyed, making place for the new world order (Rev.20:7-15, 21:1).

After that a new heaven and new earth come into being with the New Jerusalem as the Capital City (Rev.21:2-27). The New Jerusalem is brought close to the new earth with ease of access. It is the dwelling place of God and the Lamb and millions, if not billions of glorified human beings.

The new earth will also be occupied and ruled over by glorified human beings who will have access to the new capital city. Since the New Jerusalem is the dwelling place of God, it is also the administrative center of the universe, not just earth.

CHAPTER 6

THE OUTSIDERS

The following quote deals with two groups of people—the insiders and the outsiders. One group is given access and dwelling in the eternal city, the New Jerusalem; the other will not as much as see the city, given access to it nor dwell in it. It is only for registrants of the book of life. This is the Word of the Lord:

> Blessed are those who wash their robes, that they may have the right to the tree of life and may go through the gates into the city. Outside are the dogs, those who practice magic arts, the sexually immoral,

the murderers, the idolaters, and everyone who loves and practice falsehood (Rev.22:14-15 NIV).

Until now, we have been mostly focused on the insiders, the people of God, those that will dwell in the New Jerusalem or have access to the city from whatever part of the new earth they dwell. You may also notice that we have been parked in the book of Revelation a long time; now we are in the epilogue of the book. The preceding quote is six verses from the end of the book and the Bible itself.

It is Jesus talking, so it is written in red in some Bibles. Just reading it gives me a feeling of trepidation, because I know the book is about to close six short verses later. The Lord has nothing more to say after those six verses.

He gives a beatitude, a blessing to his people: "Blessed are those who wash their robes, that they may have the right to the tree of life and may go through the gates of the city" (v.14). The New King James Version (NKJV) translates, "Blessed are those who do His commandments..." for "Blessed are those who wash their robes." These are the insiders, the in group, the glorified ones.

I want to believe that I am part of the insider group, and I am happy for all of us who are in this group. But I have mixed feelings. Frankly, I have a heavy, stressful feeling in my stomach for the outside group as I write this. And I am asking myself, why do I feel like this? Perhaps, it is the next verse that triggers this loathsome feeling. It says, "Outside are the dogs, those who practice magic arts, the sexually immoral, the murderers, the idolaters, and everyone who loves and practice falsehood" (v.15).

These seven categories of people are unbelievers; they are forever lost. They are the ones who were tried at the *White Throne Judgment* and thrown into the lake of burning sulfur (Rev.20:11-15).

They join Satan, the Antichrist, the False prophet, demons, and all fallen angels thrown into the same place (Rev.19:20, 20:10).

But our concern is the human outsiders. They will never enter through the gates of the New Jerusalem. They will never see God or be able to walk into the throne room and talk to King Jesus. They will never fellowship with the millions of brethren from every nation, race, culture, and language. They will never have a sit-down chat with an angel, or walk on the streets of gold, nor dip their feet in the river of the water of life or eat from the tree of life. They are forever lost, eternally lost. They are all unbeliever catalogue under seven different sinful lifestyles. We will look at all seven briefly.

I must confess that my contemplation of the human outsider question gives me a feeling of trepidation. I am rhetorically asking, why? How will I feel then, if I am allowed to see the Lake of Fire and see the eternally lost ones? Will new creation people be able to view the eternal prison of the outsiders? Will there be more outsiders than insiders? This chapter will discuss these questions and more as we focus on the outsiders, the forever lost ones.

Seven Categories of Outsiders

There are many catalogs of lifestyle groups in the New Testament (NT) that will not inherit the kingdom of God, and no catalog by itself is comprehensive or exhaustive. To arrive at a comprehensive list or catalog, a person would have to compile a master list from all the lists or catalogs. That would call for a book of some size; that is not the purpose of this book.

We have already looked at three such lists or catalogs in Chapter 3 of this book and found that the contents of each list are closely matched, but not an exact duplicate.

In the following table (Fig.1), the apostle John provides two lists or catalogs that fall in the context of the new world order. These two lists are closely related; one has eight (8) items, the other six (6). Items #1, #2, and #3 (cowardly, unbelieving, abominable) could be all classified as unbelieving, thus making the two list even closer with six (6) items on each list. We could add unbelieving to the other side to ensure nothing is left out. Of course, from a biblical perspective everyone on the list is an unbeliever (see Fig.1 below).

Rev.21:8 (NKJV) - John	Rev.22:15 (NKJV)
1. Cowardly	1. The dogs
2. Unbelieving	2..Sorcerers (magic arts
3. Abominable (NIV -vile)	3. Sexually immoral
4. Murderers	4. Murderers
5. Sexually immoral	5. Idolaters
6. Idolaters	6. Liars
7. Sorcerers (NIV-magic arts	Add (Unbelieving) here.
8. All liars	

Now less compare our new list of seven items with the following table (Fig.2); the apostle Paul's list (1 Corinthians 6: 9-10 NKJV).

1 Cor.6:9-10 – Apostle Paul	Rev.22:15 –Apos. John
1. The unrighteous	1.Unbelievers (added)
2. Fornicators	2. The dogs
3. Homosexual	3. Sorcerers
4. Adulterer	4. Sexually immoral
5. Sodomites	5. Murderers
6. Idolaters	6. Idolaters
7. Thieves	7. Liars
8. Covetous	
9. Drunkards	
10.Revilers	
11. Extortioners	

The apostle Paul's list is longer; it has 11 items. And yet it does not include some items on John's list and vice versa. Paul's #1 (the unrighteous) is a general term like the unbelieving on John's list; it applies to everyone on the list. Paul's #2,#3,#4, and #5 are all sexually immoral. Paul's #7, #8, #11 are technically the same. A covetous person is a thief at heart; in his heart he desires his neighbor's property and will take it at the opportune time if he can.

An extortioner is a thief. Today we call them scammers; they range from the petty to the sophisticated thief. They are white-collar, blue-collar thieves, and sometimes no collar at all, just shirtless hacks in a basement somewhere with a computer. Paul's *drunkards* and *revilers* are closely associated. Reveling include several sinful behaviors: drunkenness, debauchery, lewdness, sexual activities, and the like.

Since the apostle John's list of seven item is the last to appear in the Bible, lets' give each item a definition:

- **The unbeliever**: this is the person that rejects Jesus Christ as his Savior and Lord. That's all it takes to be excluded from the kingdom of God and Christ—John 3:3-5, 14-18.
- **The dogs**: used in reference to unclean and profane people, false teachers, and preachers; people who turn others away from the from the faith – Philippians 3:2, Rev.22:15. In the time of Christ, Jews used it in reference to gentiles, Matthew 15:26.
- **Sorcerers**: Also called magic arts or witchcraft. The Bible has a lot to say about it; God always opposed it. The false profit Balaam practiced it (Numbers 22:5-41; Joshua 13:22). King Saul consulted a Witch when he could not hear from God; he lost his life (1Samuel 28:7-4). People

who practice witchcraft or sorcery are connected to demon spirits; it is used to hurt people. It is considered wickedness (Acts 8:8-23). From Bible Days life never go well for these people; God set His face against them.
- **The Sexually immoral**: this consist of a long list of deprave practices which includes fornication, adultery, homosexuality, bestiality, and the like (Gen.19:1-29; Romans 1: 20-32; 1Corinthians 6:9-10, Revelation 22:15).
- **Murderers**: A person who willfully takes the life of another. Murder is an act of premeditation (Ex.20:13; Rev.22:15). True manslaughter is the killing of a person that was never intended; there is no malice; it is an accident. In human courts a person can lie and get off with manslaughter, but if guilty, God see it as murder.
- **Idolaters**: this is the person who devote his or her life serving things or people over God (Ex.20:1-4).
- **All Liars**: Lying or false witness covers a wide range of activities that misrepresent the truth. It is intended to mislead and hurt people (Ex.20:16; Acts 5, Rev.21:8, 22:15).

At the risk of being redundant let me emphasize, people can repent of any sin and be saved; that is why Jesus came, to save lost people (Matt.1:21). But repent means you must turn away from the practice of the sin; the thief must stop stealing, the liar stop lying. The person who practices any sin as a lifestyle and refuses to repent and turn away from it and dies in that condition is lost. That person becomes a permanent outsider of the kingdom of God (1 John 3 4-10). He or she is not born-again (John 3:16). Sometimes I hear people say, "but I don't believe that!" The talk as if their unbelief makes it not to be so. You not believing the Word of God does not change anything; you only put yourself at more risk.

The Outsiders Examined

Now that we have an idea of those that will not inherit the kingdom of God, the outsiders, let us examine the term "outsiders "more closely. Where does it come from, and what does it truly mean?

First, where does it come from? The term is drawn from Revelation 22:14-15 which says, "Blessed are those who wash their robes, that they may have the right to the tree of life and may go through the gates into the city. But outside are the dogs…."

There are two groups here: the insider group who are the righteous; they are the privileged group. They are dwellers of the new heaven, the New Jerusalem, and the new earth. They have access to and from the capital city. These are the born-again, glorified group; many will have high positions in the administration of God and Christ with titles of King, Priest, and Lord among others.

Second, there are the outsiders. We know they are the ones who lived for sin, pleasure, and served Satan all their lives, and died in that lifestyle serving Satan. They were warned all the days and years of their life of the consequences and offered a way out, but they mocked and laughed and died in their chosen way.

In Revelation (20:11-15) they were resurrected, face judgment, and sentenced to the eternal lake of burning sulfur; this is the second death (Hell). The word of God declares, "For the wages of sin is death, but the gift of God is eternal life through Jesus Christ our Lord (Ro.6:23). They rejected eternal life when they rejected the Lord Jesus Christ as their Savior (John 3:16-18).

The choice we all have during our lifetime is a choice between eternal life and eternal death. If heaven were a six-month vacation, then it would be fair or just that Hell be six months as well. But the choice is between eternal life and eternal death; we all get what we sign up for, and God is not to be blamed for the choices we make. God is righteous and just in the whole matter whether we think so or not. We had our fun in sin, now we face the music.

Why did God become man in the person of Jesus Christ? He came to offer His life as a sacrifice to save us from death and hell. The plan works well saving millions, if not billions of humans, but some people reject God's plan of salvation, and elect to save themselves, do it their own way. In their pride they want to say, "I did it my way," as the popular song says. But if we can save ourselves, then God has made a colossal mistake sending His Son to die for us (Isa.53:1-12; John 3:16, 19:1-42). A drowning man has a 99.99% better chance saving himself from drowning, but zero chance saving himself from sin, death, and hell. He needs a Savior, and God has provided One (John 3:16). But some people say, No!

Jesus rose from the dead, returned to heaven, sent the blessed Holy Spirit to empower humans to deliver the good news of salvation to every nation, race, and culture that forgiveness, salvation, and eternal life is available to all (Matt.28:18-20; Acts 1:8, 2:1-48). Jesus Himself stated that this gospel must be preached as a witness to all nations before the end of the age (Matt.24:14).

He has waited two thousand years to ensure that every nation has a fair chance to hear the gospel message. Sinc then there has been many global missionary movements and the invention of faster means of travel and communication.

We have progressed from the horse-drawn carriage to the jet plane, from sailing ships to massive, motorized ships, from running a message on horseback to movable types for the printed page, to satellite communication, mass-media, social-media, the Internet, to instant communication. The gospel message is everywhere!

The gospel has been and is being preached to the far-flung regions of the world. Some individuals may have heard it ten thousand times in their lifetime and said, yes or no. If they said, yes, salvation has come to that life; but they said, no, they abide in death, eternal death (John 3:16-18). You cannot say no and have a yes outcome; eternal life is a sober, intentional choice we make.

People complain saying, from a child I heard that Jesus is coming soon, and now I am a grown adult of advance age and Jesus is not here yet. In rhetorical factiousness they ask, has He delayed His coming, or He is just caught in a traffic jam? They make fun of what is a clear blessing. The critic speaks as if Jesus had given them a set date for His return. His delay, if it is a delay, gives us more time to bring more lost souls into the kingdom from Broadway to the straight and Narrow Way.

Broadway and Narrow Way

When I speak about the outsiders, I am quietly thinking of two things: 1) will there be more outsiders than insiders, or the other way around? 2) Will the insiders be able to view the place of demise or where the outsiders are? I must warn you this is scary thinking, but worth contemplating. Let's unpack question one.

Jesus is the King of the kingdom, God incarnate. He came from heaven to surrender His life to save us. That suggest two things to me: heaven is so good that He does not want one human being to miss out on going there, or hell is so scary that He does not want one human being going there, or both.

The fact that He came to seek and to save lost humanity suggest both, He does not want us to miss heaven or go to hell. But despite the salvation plan He provides at the cost of His life, some people, if not many, will still go to hell because they refused to be saved. Jesus once said, "...wide is the gate and broad is the road that leads to destruction, and many enter through it. But small is the gate and narrow the road that leads to life, and only a few find it" (Matt.7:13-14 NIV). *Note, many one way, few the other way.*

One must be careful drawing conclusion from only one passage of scripture, but it does appear from the preceding scripture quote that the outsider's' road has more than the insider's way. Given the current (2023) population of the world of little over 8 billion people, more than half would be on the broad road. This means the Church has a lot of evangelization work to do.

So, what appears to be a delay of Christ return to some is an advantage to others to evangelize. This brings us to the classic story of Jesus and the Samaritan woman (John 4). Jews normally bypass Samaria because of ethnic prejudice. But on this day Jesus said, I must need go through Samaria (v.4). On that mission He encountered the Samaritan woman at the well; she was very lost, but Jesus sought for her and found her.

But when the disciples, who had gone to town to buy food came back, their ethnic bias got the better of them. They marveled that Jesus would be talking to a Samaritan woman (vv.27-30). To them she was low trash to be avoided, but to Jesus she was a lost soul in need of redemption. The disciples saw one woman, but Jesus saw the whole Samarian nation. Jesus said to them, "Don't you have a saying, It's four months until harvest? "[But] I tell you, open your eyes and look at the fields! They are ripe for harvest" (vv.35-36). This is a call to the Church to get busy with the work of the kingdom for we are running out of time.

The Church has a a mandate to reduce the amount of human traffic on broad way. If you are running out of reapers—Jesus said, Pray to the Lord of the harvest to send more reapers in His harvest field (Matt.9:35-38). If we end up with more outsiders than insiders, it is not because Jesus did not die for them; it is not because the new heaven, the new earth, and the new Jerusalem did have space for them, they ended up outside because the Church did not do its job of evangelization well. His delay should not be the cause for self-complacency, but an opportunity to serve more urgently. We started this section with two questions, we will answer the second in the following section.

Outsiders Prison Out of View?

The second question is this, will the dwellers or insiders of the new heaven, new earth, and new Jerusalem be able to see or visit the place where Satan and those with him are being tormented day and night? I mean, will this maximum-security secure prison where Outsiders are kept be a kind of tourist attraction? It is an uncomfortable question, sounds a little morbid, so why bring it up?

Here is why I bring it up. Revelation 22: 14-15 says, "Blessed are those who wash their robes, that they may have the right to the tree of life and may go through the gates into the city" (v.14). These are the righteous who dwell in the city (the New Jerusalem) as well as on the New earth. Remember, the New Jerusalem is suspended over the new earth with twelve (12) gates that are always open so that earth dwellers have freedom of access anytime.

But verse 15 goes on to say, "Outside are the dogs, those who practice magic arts, the sexually immoral, the murderers, the idolaters, and everyone that loves and practices falsehood." These people are in the lake of burning sulfur with Satan and his cohorts.

This is a literal place, but we do not know its location because the old earth that contained underworld of Hades (Shaol) and perhaps the Lake of burning sulfur were destroyed before the new heaven and earth are created (Rev.20:11-15,21:1-4).

Others say, the Lake of burning sulfur is eternal hell that will burn forever without destroying the spirit beings because they cannot be destroyed in the sense of taken out of existence. The Bible says it is a place where the worms die not nor the fire quenched (Mark 9:47-48).

The location therefore could be somewhere on another planet or at a place known only to God. The information is classified and will be of no concern to glorified humans in the New World order. Isaiah gives us the following intelligence report in advance:

> See, I will create a new heaven and a new earth. The former things will not be remembered, nor will they come to mind. But be glad and rejoice forever in what I will create, for I will create Jerusalem to be a delight and its people a joy. I will rejoice over Jerusalem and take delight in my people; the sound of weeping and crying will be heard in it no more. (Isaiah 65:17-19)

Part of the preceding prophecy continues beyond verse nineteen (v.19) and has reference to the millennial reign of Christ and the earthly Jerusalem. But the beginning part of the prophecy that is quoted falls withing the context of the new heaven and the new earth and applies to the New Jerusalem as well. It is a prophecy with double reference.

God will scrub our minds clean of the former things, we will not see them, hear about them, and they will never come to mind. Nothing will abridge our eternal joy and rejoicing. Thanks be to God our Father and our Savior Jesus Christ, and the Blessed Holy Spirit. Amen!

Summary

The aim of chapter six (6) is not to unnecessarily dwell on any one sin, for all sins are offensive to God, and will inevitably lead to eternal death, if not repented of. But all sins are not the same. Sins are crimes against His Majesty's government with different levels of severity of punishment. Some sins are an abomination to God and Scripture keep reminding us that people who commit them will not inherit the kingdom of God. For example, 1Corinthians 6:9-10. But if people repent, they are taken off the condemned list (v.11).

The final book of the Bible, Revelation, closed with two list of these people that will not enter the Kingdom (Rev.21:8, 22:15). We find that these two lists are consistent with lists that appear throughout the Bible, though not exact duplicates of each other.

We further found that those that will not inherit the kingdom of God are called outsiders (Rev.22:14-15). We wanted to find out if the insiders will be able to view the outsiders in their place of punishment. The conclusion is no; the place of punishment is classified. It is known and accessible only to God. But this is more of an intelligent opinion, not explicit scripture.

The former way of life will be scrub clean from the minds of glorified people who occupy the new heaven, new earth, and in the New Jerusalem there will be no bad memory of our former earthly, the former things are scrub clean from our minds; nothing will abridge our eternal joy and new way of life (Isa.65:17-19).

CHAPTER 7

SECURING YOUR DWELLING IN THE NEW JERUSALEM

Who among us would not want to have a mansion and a leadership position in the new world order? Who would not want to have the right to enter through the Pearly Gates of the New Jerusalem, walk on its streets of pure gold, eat the succulent fruits of the Tree of Life, and dangle your feet in the refreshing waters of the River of Life? Who would not want to sit face to face with His Majesty, the KING of King, in the throne room of God and Christ? Well, all that and more can be secured right now in time, before we take our final breath in the body and time changes to eternity.

What do you have to do now to secure this kind of future for yourself? That information may have been a well-kept secret, but no more. This chapter tells you plainly what you must do now to secure that kind of eternity. This is the most important chapter in the whole book, because it gives you the key to the eternal city. Nobody can hinder you from a dwelling place fully paid for in that city of gold but the person between your two arms. Perhaps, the sun should not go down this day before you take the necessary steps to secure your dwelling.

One Way to Secure Entrance

The eternal city, the New Jerusalem, is the capital city of the kingdom of God; it is where God and His people will live (Rev.21:1-7). We gain entrance and secure our place in the city through a salvation experience and relationship with Jesus Christ only.

Jesus Himself made this clear when He said to a Jewish teacher, a rabbi, "No one can see the kingdom of God unless he is born again" (John 3:1-4). Jesus goes on to say, "...no one can enter the kingdom of God unless they are born of water and of the Spirit" (v.5). The key words here are "enter the kingdom." You do not wait until you die to enter the kingdom. It will be too late then; you have lost your chance to secure your dwelling place. Your future is dark!

Jesus is the King of the kingdom to which you seek entrance, so He of all persons should know how you get in, what the admissions requirements are. He said, "you must be born again."

But what does He mean by being "born again" by "water and of the Spirit?" This means a spiritual birth, a birth from above through the agency of "water" and "Spirit." Water represents the Word of God. Some scholars say, means baptism, but the preferred meaning is the Word of God. Hear what the apostle Peter who walked with Jesus says, "For you have been born again, not of perishable seed, but of imperishable, through the living word of God" (1Peter 1:23). So, water baptism, though important is not what get you born again or saved; it is the Word of God. But that is not all.

Jesus said, "You must be born of the water and of the Spirit." What does He mean by "Spirit?" Spirit refers to the Holy Spirit. The Word of God and the Holy Spirit are the two agents at work bringing about the miracle of the new birth. You can be a sinner bound for hell one moment and the next moment bound for heaven, like the dying thief on the cross who said to Jesus, "Jesus, remember me when you come into your kingdom" (Luke 23 32,39-43). By looking to Jesus and asking for help he immediately gained entrance into the kingdom, for Jesus said to him, "Truly I tell you, today you will be with me in Paradise" (v.43). He is changed from sinner to saint!

When a person gets saved, he or she hears the Word of God preached and the Holy Spirit use the spoken or written word to bring about conviction in the person's heart, moving him or her to repentance. He or she asks for forgiveness and receives Jesus as his Savior and Lord. It is at this point that we say the person is born again, saved, or converted, all mean the same thing. At that moment, your name is registered in the *Book of Life* in heaven, and your walk with the Lord begins (Luke 15:1-10; Heb.12:22-24).

But note well—there is no other person or way in all of creation to secure your place in the kingdom of God, but the way shown to you here. You must have a salvation experience with Jesus Christ if you want the gift of eternal life (John 3:16; Rom.6:23). Jesus told His disciples that He was returning to heaven to prepare a place for them in His Father's house (John 14:1-4). Secure your place.

One disciple asked, "How will we get there, since we don't know the way?" Jesus said, "I am the way and the truth and the life. No one comes to the father except through me" (v.6). Jesus is the only way into the kingdom of God; to secure a place in the eternal city one must have a salvation relationship with Him. This fact is repeated numerous times in the Bible, the Word of God.

Furthermore, this born-again, salvation relationship must be established while you are alive in the body. If you die in your sins, not establishing this relation with Jesus Christ, you are forever lost. You will not have a relationship in the kingdom of our Lord or a dwelling place in His kingdom. You cannot repent after death; no pastor, bishop, priest, or pope can change your destiny after death.

I must emphasize that it is not religion or religious activities that get you into heaven; it is a born-again relationship with Jesus, the Son of God. If you have this experience, you are in. Next, we will build on this foundation, or relationship to secure your dwelling place in the eternal city.

Building on the Foundation

All genuine, authentic candidates for the kingdom gained entrance at the same starting point, they are born again (John 3:1-5). Being born again is a spiritual birth from above.

Being born again can be compared with physical birth as Jesus did (John 3:1-18). We all came into the natural world through physical birth. You did not just join your family or this world; you were born into it. The same is true with the kingdom of God. You can't just join a church and think you are automatically in the kingdom of God and a member of God's family. You must be born again into it. But this is a spiritual birth from above (vv.6-8).

Being born again is starting a relationship with Jesus Christ. It is a foundational experience normally followed by water baptism and fellowship with a local body of believers (Matt.28:19-20; Acts 2:38-47). You have begun a new lifestyle, a journey, and your guidebook is the Word of God. Always check what you are told in the book to see if it is so or not so. Have one good, experienced spiritual mentor that you trust and respect to guide you; this person's life must bear evidence that he or she is a genuine child of God, not a hypocrite, not a fraud.

You will encounter many false, opinionated, and misguided travelers on the road, some of them in religious vestment. But compare the life they live with the book and check out what they say with the book to see if it is so. No one has the authority to overrule the book, not bishop, not pastors, not popes or cardinals. Yes, at times you will need trusted, wise, Spirit filled counsel. Be sure it is in keeping with the Word of God.

The person who wants to secure his or her place in the New Jerusalem must build on his born-again experience; it is a growing spiritual experience. The Bible says, "...grow in grace and in the knowledge of our Lord and Savior Jesus Christ" (2 Peter 3:18). Here are a few suggestions to help you secure your dwelling in the eternal city.

1. **Keep your eyes on eternity.** In other words, don't allow the present cultures of this world to shape your life; the kingdom of God has its own culture (Roman 12: 1-2). Many of the lifestyles that the world embrace are ungodly, sinful, and your guidebook tells you the people who practice these lifestyles will not inherit the kingdom of God (1Corinthians 6:9-10). They will be shutout of the eternal

city (Revelation 21:8, 22:14-15). The born-again lifestyle is lived according to the book.

It does not mean that you are going to hate the people who live the lifestyles of this world. No, you show them Christian love, patience, and tolerance. That way you can influence them in love to change. But you cannot approve of those lifestyles, but your disapproval cannot be mean and hateful. It must be Christlike.

Jesus was gentle with the woman that a religious mob was ready to stone to death for adultery. Jesus did not condone adultery, but He saved her life from the religious haters (John 8:1-11). He did the same for the woman at the well; He did not condone her lifestyle, but he treated her with respect, kindness, and gentleness (John 4:1-26, 39-42).

2. Value spiritual things over material things. The material things of this world are here for our enjoyment. God does not mind you having money, a good house, a good car, clothes, good-paying job, a good vacation, and an excellent retirement package. He wants you to have these things and more, but he does not want them to have you. You should not be preoccupied with them; they should not be your priority. They should not become your God (Matt.6:25-34). The righteousness of Christ and the business of His kingdom should be your preoccupation (v.33).

One of the reasons the Lord does not want us to be preoccupied with material things is the fact that they are not lasting; they will leave us, or we will leave them. In Luke 12 (vv.13-21) Jesus tells the story of the rich fool who was preoccupied with material goods but had no time for things spiritual. His life was snatched in his prime at high noon. He had neither wife nor children, who then will get those things, Jesus asked? But he must now face God empty handed. He is a fool not because he was rich; he is a fool because material thing became his God (v.21). He is no fool let go of the things he cannot keep, and cling to the thing he cannot lose.

3. *Do some of your banking in heaven*. This is spiritual talk which means there are certain earthly things that are of value in heaven; the more of them that we do are credited to our account in heaven. Some of these things are truth, compassion, kindness, mercy, forgiveness, and the like these are deposit or pluses. Where lying, theft, false witness, adultery, hate, cruelty are minuses.

Concerning banking in heaven Jesus gives us this advice:

> Do not store up for yourselves treasures on earth, where moths and vermin destroy, and where thieves break in and steal. But store up for yourselves, treasures in heaven, where moths and vermin do not destroy, and where thieves do not break in and steal. For where your treasure is, there your heart will be also. (Matthew 6: 19-21)

What is the quote really saying? It is saying that spiritual things are a more lasting and safe investment; they have eternal values in this world and the world to come. The person with more of this wealth is the one who is rich toward God. Some people are bereft of spiritual things, they will not make it into heaven at all.

4. *Serve Christ in Love, not Self*. One attribute of people who are authentically born again is that they serve Jesus Christ in love, not themselves. There are many people who are in ministry for different reasons, and honoring Christ is not one of them. They use the name of the Lord dishonestly, to enrich themselves. If they are saved, they will enter heaven, but they will receive no reward at the Believers Judgment (2 Corinthians 5:10). Their works will go up in flames, but they will be saved (1Corinthians 3:10-15). (See Vol.2).

To command a great place of leadership in the new world order, we must show faithfulness in our stewardship here and now (Matthew 25:14-30). Note in this story that the key for being given greater responsibility in the world to come is our faithfulness to Christ now. The great apostle Paul is looking for a crown of righteousness from Jesus Christ on the day of judgment (2 Timothy 4:6-8). Why? Because he felt he was faithful in the assignment Christ gave him. What does a crown symbolize? Kingship, leadership. We secure our place of prominence in the world to come by serving Christ faithfully in this present world.

5. *Serving God by serving people*. Greatness in the kingdom of God is very different from greatness in the kingdoms of this world. In this world greatness is seen in how well we are served; it is about us, so we impress people with our entourage of servants.

Speaking of kingdom of God and Himself Jesus said, "the Son of Man came not to be served but to serve, and to give his life a ransom for many" (Matt.20:28). Greatness is not ruling over others but serving them in love.

When we serve others in love in the name of the Lord, that is considered a service to God. In Matthew 25 (vv.31-46) the judgment is depicted as dividing the nations into two camps: sheep and goats. To the sheep on His right hand, He say:

> Come, you who are blessed by my Father; take your inheritance, the kingdom prepared for you since the creation of the world. For I was hungry, and you gave

me something to eat, I was thirsty and you gave me something to drink, I was a stranger and you took me in, I need clothes and you clothed me, I was sick and you looked after me, I was in prison and you came to see me. (Matthew 25:34-36)

When the righteous heard all the good things credited to them, they were really surprised and asked, Lord when did we do these good things for you? The Lord responded, "Truly, I tell you, whatever you did for one of the least of these brothers and sisters of mine, you did for me" (vv.37-40). These people rose to the opportunity to compassionately serve others when it was in their power to do so. They were serving God without realizing it.

The people on the Lord's left hand, the goats, are all guilty of doing the very opposite. They lack compassion for people and did not rise to serve others when it was in their power to do so; for that cruelty, they are disinherited (vv.41-46). If they had a been born again into the kingdom, they no doubt would have acted in a Christlike manner, with compassion. Good works alone are not enough to save anyone, you must also be born again.

A good illustration of good works versus salvation is the story of Cornelius (Acts 10). By profession, Cornelius was a gentile, a centurion of the Roman army based at Caesarea. He was in charge of one hundred soldiers. Religiously, he was a good who feared the God of Israel, a generous man to the poor, a philanthropist. His good works got the attention of God, and an angel was sent to him at his house to tell him where to find a man named, Simon Peter, who would explain the way of salvation to him.

He sent men to call Simon Peter who was in another city called, Jappa. God knows that Peter is a Jew and would not readily visit the home of a gentile, so God had to prepare Peter in advance of the arrival of the men from Cornelius. They arrived and Peter went with them. By this time Cornelius had several of his family members at his house awaiting Peter's arrival.

Peter arrived and explained the way of salvation by talking about Jesus Christ who died for our sins and rose again from the dead, and how forgiveness of sin and eternal life is available to all in the name of Jesus.

While Peter was still talking, the Holy Spirit fell on all who were gathered and fill them as it first happened to Peter and the rest of the apostles on the day of Pentecost (Acts 2:1-46). Peter baptized Cornelius and his household in water. Peter was dumbfounded.

There are three things, I want to highlight from this all-important story in the life of the early Church and Simon Peter:

(1) God is no respecter of persons. He overruled Peters prejudice culture to bring him to the house of a gentile that Peter would not go under ordinary circumstances.

(2) God love good works of charity, but it is not enough to save you. You must come to know Jesus Christ to receive salvation and forgiveness of sin. You cannot bypass Jesus and get into heaven, no matter how good you are.

(3) The preaching of the gospel is not entrusted to angels; this assignment is given to humans (Matthew 28:16-20; Acts 1:8). If you read these two references from the Bible, you will see that the assignment given by Jesus to preach the gospel crosses all barriers national, racial, cultural, and more. But our ethnic biases can get in the way.

Summary

We began this chapter with the question of how to secure our dwelling place in the new world order, on the new earth, and in the New Jerusalem. It is an issue that all human beings should carefully consider. What we do in this life has tremendous impact upon our status in the world to come. Therefore, we should not just spend the days of our life being preoccupied with material things that we cannot keep. *We should keep our eyes on eternity,* consciously and carefully building a lasting future there.

We should not be like the rich fool who valued material things over things spiritual that he lived a life that was unbalanced. He had all of one thing and none of the other, and what he had was without eternal value. One had a temporary shelf life in terms of value, the other had value that paid eternal dividends. We should do some off shore banking in heaven where thieves do not brake in and steal, and where moth and rust do not corrupt, and where our treasure is, our hearts will be also.

A strong point we learn is to serve God by serving people in love. In the judgment of nations, people are given the right of way to enter the kingdom because they served Jesus by serving people (Matt.25:31-46). When the King returns, the King whose kingdom you seek entrance and eternal dwelling-- divides people into two camps: sheep and goats.

Those who gain entrance to His kingdom are those with compassion, who serve others in love. He said, "I was hungry and you fed me, I was naked and you clothed me, I was sick and you cared for me." When did we see you and provided such assistance to you Jesus? His response to your question in as much as you have done it to the least of these my brethren, you have done it unto me. Come into my kingdom and share my joys.

He turns to those on His left hand and said depart from me, you workers of iniquity, prepare for the devil and his angels. Because I was hungry, and you did not feed me. I was thirsty and you gave me nothing to drink. I was sick and you did not care for me. I was naked and you did not clothe me. In as much as you did not do it for these the lease of my brethren, you did not do it for me.

The person that has a salvation relation with Jesus Christ share His values and manifest the culture of the kingdom of God. You have compassion for people. These are the ways to secure your dwelling place in the New Jerusalem.

REFERENCES

Chapter 1

1. Berkhof, Louis. *Systematic Theology, New Combined Edition.* Grand Rapids, MI: William B. Eerdmans Publishing Company, Vol.2, 29.

2. Richter, Sandrea L. *Steward of Eden: What Scripture Says About the Environment and Why Its Matters.* Downers Grov, IL: InterVarsity Press, 2020, 5-14.

Chapter 2

1. Pawson, David. The Road to Hell, Everlasting Torment or Annihilation? Travelers Rest, SC: True Potential Publishers, Inc., 2007, 75-76.

2. NASA, https://spaceplace.nasa.gov/exosphere.

3. National Geographic, https://education.nationalgeographic.org/resource/atmosphere.

4. Pawson, David. *The Road to Hell*, 85.

5. Sproul, R.C. *Unseen Realities, Heaven, Hell, Angels and Demons.* Ligonier Ministries. Lake Mary, FL. 2011, 40-41.

6. Halley, Henry H. *Halley's Bible Handbook. Deluxe Edition.* Grand Rapids, MI: Zondervanm, 2007, 886.

Chapter 3

1. Unger, Merrill F. "Spiritual Inheritance" in, *The New Unger's Bible Dictionary.* Chicago, IL: Moody Bible Institute, 1988, 618.

2. *The New Unger's Bible Dictionary.* "Adoption," **85.**

Chapter 4

1. Sproul, R.C. *Unseen Realities, Heaven, Hell, Angels and Demons.* Ligonier Ministries. Lake Mary, FL. 2011, 139-147

2. Ibid.

OTHER BOOKS BY THIS AUTHOR

Vol.1

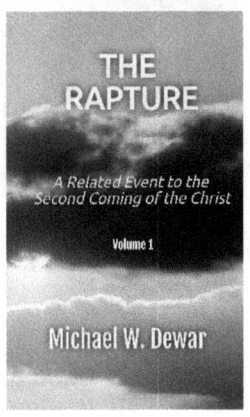

Vol. 2

Vol.3

Vol.4

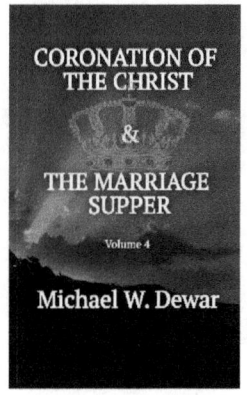

Vol.5

Vol.6

Vol.7

Vol.8

OTHER BOOKS BY THIS AUTHOR

Vol. 9   **Vol.10**

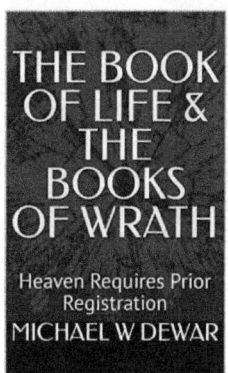

A three-volume training course to establish a peace ministry in your curch: Textbook, Instructor's Manual, and Students' Manual. Train them to become Ministers of Peace- Managers of Conflicts.

Instructor's Manual   **Students' Manual**

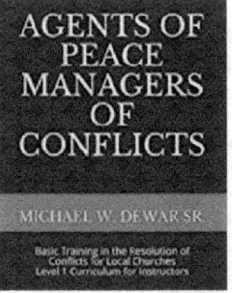 

ABOUT THE AUTHOR

Michael W. Dewar, Sr. is a pastor, Bible teacher, and mentor in the spiritual life. He is a Licensed Mater Social Worker, and a specialist in conflict management and resolution, including church and family conflicts. He trains Agents of Peace-Managers of Conflicts to launch peace ministries in local churches.

Reverend Dewar is the founder and pastor of the New York Congregational Baptist Church (NYCBC), and the author of several books, including a tree-volume training course on Church and Family Conflicts.

He holds earned degrees from several institutions of higher learning, including the Master of Divinity from what is now Palmer Theological Seminary, Eastern University, the Master of Social Work from Wurzweiler School of Social Work, Yeshiva University, the LMSW from the State of New York, and a doctorate from Regent University, School of Divinity.

At the time of this publication, Reverend Dewar pastors in New York where he lives with his family.

"Look, I am coming soon! My reward is with me, and I will give to each person according to what he has done" (Rev.22!2 NIV).

CONTACT AND REVIEW

If this book has been a blessing to you, I would appreciate an honest review from you. Go to: Amazon.com/Customer Review/ and search for the book you which to do a review on, one book at a time. Be sure the name of the author and the title of the book correctly.

===============

If you have feedback that would improve the quality of the book, submit your feedback me (the author) at: CS@DPSCleansing.com Be sure to include the title of the book, volume number, and clearly state your suggestion.

===============

To purchase all 10 books in the series at once (eBooks). Go to Amazon.com and search for this: **B0B4TDK1QJ**. You may have to buy the paperback one at a time.

===============

Join mailing list from website here or copy and paste this in your browser: DPSCleansing.com.

"Look, I come soon! Blessed is the one who keeps the words of the prophecy written in this scroll" (Rev.22:7 NIV).

THE NEW WORLD ORDER

www.ingramcontent.com/pod-product-compliance
Lightning Source LLC
Chambersburg PA
CBHW071717040426
42446CB00011B/2096